PHILADELPHIA STORIES
A *Photographic* History, 1920–1960

Fredric M. Miller

Morris J. Vogel

Allen F. Davis

PHILADELPHIA STORIES

A
Photographic
History,
1920–1960

Temple University Press

Philadelphia

Temple University Press, Philadelphia 19122
Copyright © 1988 by Temple University. All rights reserved
Published 1988
Printed in the United States of America
Maps by Karen L. Wysocki

Designed by Arlene Putterman

The paper used in this publication
meets the minimum requirements of
American National Standard for Information
Sciences—Permanence of Paper for
Printed Library Materials, ANSI Z39.48-1984

Library of Congress Cataloging-in-Publication Data
Miller, Fredric.
    Philadelphia stories: a photographic history, 1920–1960 /
Fredric M. Miller, Morris J. Vogel, and Allen F. Davis.
        p.   cm.
    Includes index.
    ISBN 0-8772-551-6
    1. Philadelphia (Pa.)—Description—Views.
2. Philadelphia (Pa.)—Social life and customs—Pictorial works.
I. Vogel, Morris J.   II. Davis, Allen Freeman. 1931–   .   Title.
F158.37.M56   1968
974.8'1104—dc19   87-37379

To our colleagues and friends at Temple University

Contents

Preface

This is another book about Philadelphia and about photographs. In some ways it is the sequel to our *Still Philadelphia* of 1983, but it can stand alone and be read, looked at, and pondered without reference to the other book. Like *Still Philadelphia*, however, it attempts to translate social history, the story of ordinary citizens of Philadelphia—their work and play, their lives and their hopes—into a visual and readable form. It is also an urban history, tracing change in the roles of the city and suburbs, their fortunes, and their very appearance.

In this book, we start with the 1920s and 1930s when Philadelphia teetered on the brink of the modern world, and yet had many characteristics of a more traditional age. We trace the story to 1960 when Philadelphia and the world had undergone radical transformations. In the process, we chart the roller coaster that took the region's industrial economy, already in decline in the 1920s, to the depths of depression in the 1930s, then to a massive revival during World War II, and the mixed success of the postwar period.

Some of the changes in Philadelphia were the result of national and international events: the Great Depression, World War II, immigration restriction, and the massive movement of southern blacks into northern cities. New technologies also left their marks on the city: automobiles and airplanes, radio and television, plastics and synthetic fibers. But other significant trends were at least in part the result of Philadelphia's peculiar history. The city's racial and ethnic mix, its unique industrial base, and its rowhouse neighborhoods meant that new national trends took longer to appear in the city.

To a greater extent than in *Still Philadelphia*, we are concerned in this volume with the impact of outside events on the city's history, and we do record such public events as the Mummers' parade, protest marches, and baseball games. We even include a photograph of Independence Hall. Yet, just as in *Still Philadelphia*, we have avoided the formal and ceremonial urban view. Our focus remains on the lives of the ordinary people of Philadelphia and what the photographs can tell us about those people and the city they lived in.

The photographs come from a number of sources. Some were taken by Farm Security Administration or WPA photographers during the 1930s and they betray the special social-documentary style of that time. A few from the Philadelphia Housing Association are in the old tradition of progressive-era photography: they document and sometimes exaggerate social ills in order to promote change. But many more of the photographs in this volume were taken by photojournalists recording strikes, parades, and human interest stories with a characteristic mixture of professional distance and technical skill.

Photojournalism was transformed in this period by a number of developments. The most important was the gradual adoption of cameras like the light-weight Leica and the larger and more versatile Rolleiflex, which allowed photographers to take candid shots without a tripod. But it was magazines rather than newspapers that led the way in the creative use of photographs. The most significant event here was the founding of *Life* on November 23, 1936 by Henry Luce, the American entrepreneur who had already launched *Time* and *Fortune*.

Life's popularity and its coverage of the news, especially its photo essays that told a human interest story, changed the way other magazines and newspapers used photographs. No longer was it good enough simply to illustrate the news. One had to have action photographs and human interest stories told with pictures. *Life* and its imitators, together with the *March of Time* newsreels started in 1935, created a revolution in the way Americans learned about the world around them. Instead of depending on print, Americans learned through photographs and the moving picture. It was a media revolution as important as that caused by television in the 1950s. There are many examples of that revolution in this book.

Some of the photographers represented here are famous—Jack Delano and Lewis Hine, for example, and there are talented amateurs such as Meyer Sherow. But most of the photographs were taken by anonymous professionals who were doing their jobs and trying to record the best and most interesting image. Yet all the pictures were taken with a point of view and a purpose, and that was just as true of the straightforward newsphoto as of the intimate pictures in the family albums in this book.

Since 1888, when Kodak developed the first inexpensive and nearly automatic camera, families have been taking candid snapshots and creating millions of informal family images. "You press the button, we do the rest," Kodak proudly announced. In 1931, a Kodak Beau Brownie camera cost four dollars, putting it within reach of most middle-class families even during the Depression. And after World War II, amateur cameras became even less expensive and easier to use.

Family photographs differ from the more formal variety taken by professional photographers. They were often out of focus, heads were cut off, and scenes strangely distorted and blurred. Yet family photos give us a special angle of vision on the past. When posing for professional photographers, one projects a certain image, a well-thought-out stance toward the world. Many family photographs are also posed, but in a different way, for usually the photographer is a family member or a close friend. Children pose for the camera and adults act self-conscious or silly, but the posturing is in an intimate and friendly context.

Some periods produced more family photos than others. World War II, for example, caused a great increase in film exposed. Every get-together might be the last, so it became important to record the occasion on film. A soldier home on leave, a wedding reception, or simply a family picnic took on added meaning. Many people used their cameras to record these moments so that they could be remembered forever. Servicemen and women carried snapshots of their loved ones to distant lands until they became frayed and faded, while those who stayed behind proudly displayed formal portraits and candid shots of those in the service. But other decades produced their memorable snapshots as well.

In the pages that follow we have provided extensive introductions and captions in an effort to interpret and tease out the meaning of photographs taken by amateurs and professionals alike. But we have by no means exhausted the possible ways of understanding these images from the past. We invite readers to go beyond our captions to find their own personal meaning in these photographs, to look and interpret them through their own memories and experiences. As we look at a photograph, we are witnessing a moment captured by the click of a shutter. Here is recorded the rich and varied material culture of a past age. Once again we invite those who share our fascination with Philadelphia and with old photographs to savor and enjoy this book, to be reminded of how things have changed— and how they have stayed the same.

Acknowledgments

A book like this can only be created through the help and cooperation of people in many institutions and repositories. We therefore extend our heartfelt appreciation to the following: John Alviti and Jeffrey Ray, Atwater Kent Museum; R. Joseph Anderson and Patricia Proscino, Balch Institute for Ethnic Studies; Ward Childs and Lee Stanley, Philadelphia City Archives; Jerry Post, Free Library of Philadelphia; Linda Stanley and Peter Parker, Historical Society of Pennsylvania; Robert Plowman, National Archives—Philadelphia Branch; Linda Ries and Roland Baumann, Pennsylvania Historical and Museum Commission; David Weinberg, Urban Archives, Temple University; and the staffs of the Print and Photograph Division of the Library of Congress and the Still Pictures Branch, National Archives. Special thanks are due to George Brightbill, Pamela Austin, and Margaret McGrath of the Photojournalism Collection of the Urban Archives, from which many of the photographs in this book are reproduced.

Hundreds of Philadelphians responded to our request for personal photographs by sharing important pieces of their lives with us. The photographs they generously sent us made possible the family albums that enrich this book. Selecting the fraction of photographs that could appear in the text was a difficult task, for we understand how meaningful these photographs are to those who offered them to us. We are deeply in their debt.

We also benefited from colleagues and friends who gave us advice and encouragement, read early drafts of the book, and shared with us their knowledge of Philadelphia and photography. We especially want to thank Leann Ayers, Dennis Clark, Kenneth Finkel, Hal Kessler, Cynthia Little, Meredith Savery, Philip Scranton, Harry Silcox, and Janis Somerville.

Zohrab Kazanjian, Richard Good, and Greg Szczepanek of Temple University's Audiovisual Center printed many of the photographs which appear here. Arnold Thomas copied many of the original prints housed at the Historical Society of Pennsylvania. We wrote the text hoping that it would live up to Arlene Putterman's obvious design skills. Finally, David Bartlett, director of the Press, played an important role in this project from its outset.

PHILADELPHIA STORIES A Photographic History, 1920–1960

Introduction: A City in Transition

In the decades between the two world wars, Philadelphia was a city balanced between the old and the new. The prosperity of the 1920s contrasted sharply with the squalor and despair of the 1930s. Yet over the course of those decades, the city of immigrants and industry, of crowded rowhouse neighborhoods and deeply rooted old world habits, was giving way perceptibly to a distinctly modern Philadelphia. The interruption of European immigration, the growth to unprecedented levels of a black population uprooted from the South, the widespread adoption of the automobile, and suburban expansion impressed the outlines of the contemporary metropolis on Philadelphia's social and physical landscape. For all the change, Philadelphia on the eve of World War II remained a traditional city, its historic patterns and ways of life accommodating to new forces, surviving both expansion and depression as the city had earlier survived the coming of industry, the introduction of streetcars, and the influx of unfamiliar immigrants.

The dramatic immigration from southern and eastern Europe that had filled the old neighborhoods, factories, and streets with new faces and strange voices slackened, then stopped, a casualty first of wartime restriction in Europe and then of American legislation in the 1920s. As the flow of newcomers dropped off, so too did the intensity with which the ways of the old world were kept alive. Immigrants who had arrived between 1880 and 1924 settled in more completely, following their children into a fuller participation in American life, adjusting to the demands and opportunities of the new world while remembering the old. Americanization slowly transformed life in the immigrant districts; its impact on their appearance was less obvious.

Physically, the oldest neighborhoods changed little. Both of Philadelphia's historic nineteenth-century slums—the area from Race north to Girard Avenue between the Delaware River and Fifth Street, and the Society Hill–South Philadelphia district from the Delaware to Eighth and Lombard to Christian—survived well into the mid-twentieth century. Living conditions were generally more wholesome in the newer industrial belts stretching along the Delaware River north of downtown and the Pennsylvania and Reading railroad lines. These historic neighborhoods continued as they long had, portals for the city's new poor, homes for its workers, havens for its destitute.

Though poor, the older neighborhoods were in many ways attractive. Well into the 1930s, guidebooks pointed out the sights and sounds of the old world encountered in the Jewish, Italian, Greek, and Chinese areas—"the special quarters [of] peoples not easily assimilated"—which

Workers on the Delaware River Bridge,
c. 1937

NORTHEAST

PHILADELPHIA

Roosevelt Blvd.

Grant Ave.

Frankford Ave.

Fox
Chase

Pennypack Cr.

Torresdale

Cottman Ave.

Oxford Ave.

Cheltenham Ave.

Stenton Ave.

Ogontz Ave.

Oak Lane

Rising Sun Ave.

Mayfair

Chest-
nut
Hill

Germantown Ave.

Chelten Ave.

Olney

Oxford
Circle

Ridge Ave.

Wissahickon Cr.

Mount Airy

Olney Ave.

Logan

Roosevelt Blvd.

Feltonville

Juniata
Park

Frankford

Bridge St.

Tacony Bridge

Roxborough

Germantown

Broad St.

Hunting
Park

Tacony Cr.

Schuylkill River

Mana-
yunk

Henry Ave.

Nicetown

Erie Ave.

Richmond St.

Brides-
burg

East
Falls

Tioga

Front St.

Lehigh Ave.

NORTH

Richmond St.

City Ave.

Wynnefield

PHILADELPHIA

Port
Richmond

Belmont Ave.

Overbrook

Strawberry
Mansion

Kensington

Delaware River

Lancaster Ave.

Girard Ave.

Parkway

Haverford Ave.

Parkside

WEST

East
Poplar

Northern
Liberties

Market St.

PHILADELPHIA

China-
town

Delaware River
Bridge

63rd St.

Cobbs
Creek

Baltimore Ave.

South St.

Society
Hill

52nd St.

Gray's
Ferry

Southwark

Woodland Ave.

Passyunk Ave.

Broad St.

Oregon Ave.

SOUTH

Island Ave.

Essington Ave.

East-
wick

PHILADELPHIA

Broad St.

gave the city a cosmopolitan charm. Life poured out onto the stoops and into the streets—this perhaps as much the result of crowding and local custom as a throwback to peasant villages. Equally colorful street vendors could also trace their origins to the city's colonial past and to the diverse backgrounds of its peoples. Blacks sold oysters and hominy from carts, the canteloupe man vied with the strawberry woman in July, and during the summer children waited for the ice cream cart with their spoons, cups, and pennies.

New and growing neighborhoods appeared along the city's periphery, drawing the established middle class outward in the 1920s to homes in such diverse communities as Oxford Circle, Oak Lane, Mount Airy, and Overbrook. Suburbs grew outside the city as well as within its boundaries, with Delaware, Montgomery, and Camden counties experiencing the most substantial growth. Lower Merion, Springfield (Montgomery County), Lansdowne, Radnor, Ridley Township, and Collingswood had population gains of more than 50 percent in the 1920s, while Collingdale, Haverford, Sharon Hill, Yeadon, Springfield in Delaware County, Abington, and Pennsauken more than doubled. Upper Darby registered an increase from 9,000 to 46,000 inhabitants, a jump unusual both in its extraordinary size and in its being a result of the elevated line rather than the automobile, a continuation of West Philadelphia's expansion across the city line rather than a distinct suburb. New phenomena, automobile-based shopping centers like Suburban Square in Ardmore, appeared to serve the more prosperous residents of the outlying communities. Elsewhere, notably Jenkintown, clusters of older shops developed identities as regional retailing centers.

Many outward migrants were moving from still-pleasant blocks in the city's original streetcar suburbs, the middle sections of North and West Philadelphia built from the late nineteenth century on. Immigrants and their children, in turn, found new homes in Strawberry Mansion, Parkside, Logan, and the more modest sections of Wynnefield, adopting an amalgam of American and old world culture to suit their new neighborhoods. Jewish Philadelphians more readily than Italians or Poles abandoned the older neighborhoods. While some Italians moved into pockets in the city's northern and western sections, most tended instead to settle more comfortably into South Philadelphia, remodeling houses on older streets and moving south and west to such newer areas as the Girard Estate. Massive landfills undertaken below Oregon Avenue to provide space for the Sesquicentennial of 1926 drew population southward, though up to the late 1940s problems with poor drainage left large areas of South and Southwest Philadelphia vacant. Only the most fortunate of the newer immigrants fully entered middle-class prosperity in the 1920s, but almost all came to live in less-crowded districts, indirect beneficiaries of the automobile-driven dispersion of population.

Philadelphia's blacks had mixed experiences with residential opportunities. The city's black population grew by 64 percent in the 1920s, the result of an extraordinary northward migration unleashed by hard times in the South and the expanding industrial economy of World War I. The influx was further fueled by the immigration-restriction acts of the 1920s, which forced industry to recruit black southerners to refill the unskilled labor pool depleted by the cut-off of European laborers. Even in the 1930s, the city's black census continued to rise—though only by 14 percent— while white population fell. Racism restricted housing availability, but the outward movement of many white residents of the rowhouse city opened some of the older streetcar neighborhoods to blacks as it did to southern and eastern Europeans. Once substantially confined to older housing along the South Street corridor and adjacent areas, blacks moved into newer and better houses in large pockets of West and North Philadelphia. Indeed, North Philadelphia—including "The Ridge," along the avenue of that name, between Broad Street and Fairmount Park—replaced the southern section of the city as the center of black Philadelphia. Even with the dramatic growth of black population, these neighborhoods were less crowded than the traditional black community. But there was another side to the transformation. Segregation based in racism had deep roots in the city, but the historic black neighborhoods had always been substantially integrated. The rigid division of black and white communities that was to characterize the mid-twentieth century was in many ways a product of the racial reapportionment of the streetcar neighborhoods that began in the 1920s.

The Great Depression halted the city's outward growth, temporarily interrupting the transformation of the physical and social landscape. Older communities continued their steady deterioration during the 1930s, and the quality of life in many neighborhoods suffered with the collapse of the economy, but the physical appearance of Depression-era Philadelphia changed little from the preceding decade. Few newcomers arrived to make their homes here, and there was little change in the ethnic or racial composition of the city's neighborhoods. Indeed, the blend of old and new that took shape in the 1920s would survive until outward growth and population dispersion resumed and racial segregation grew more rigid in the years after World War II.

In Philadelphia's oldest neigh-borhoods, the faces and scenes of the late 1930s recalled the pre-vious century. These crowded streets near downtown were the city's most genuinely integrated neighborhoods as well as its poor-est. As they had for decades, the old sections provided compelling images for those seeking to expose injustice and redress problems. An *Evening Bulletin* photographer illustrating housing problems took this shot of "Maria, her friend, and a doll carriage" on the 1200 block of Lombard Street in Janu-ary 1938. Though the immediate neighborhood was almost entirely black—St. Peter Clavier's Church, established for blacks in 1892, was across the street—the photographer evoked sympathy for the residents by focusing on these two little girls. The photograph on the next page was taken for the Philadelphia *Record* about 1937 to demon-strate the need for public housing. More representative in its sam-pling of neighborhood children, it shows a group sitting across Queen Street from St. Philip Neri Roman Catholic Church, where a narrow covered alley led into Gain's Place, a courtyard of half a dozen tiny, three-story, three-room homes. The neighborhood's mixed black, Italian, Jewish, and Polish popula-tion seems reflected in the people posing for the camera. In both photographs, the "picturesque" faces so appealing to photojournal-ists and to the newspaper public undercut the message of suffering and deprivation they were supposed to convey.

Most Philadelphians in the 1930s lived in the rowhouse neighborhoods of North, South, and West Philadelphia. Even the suburban ring was dominated by largely working-class communities like Camden, Chester, and Norristown. Most of these areas were not impoverished, but their residents had to make do on limited means. Two of these photographs vividly illustrate how some residents dealt with summer heat: Below, residents of an unidentified neighborhood cool off in June 1933 in a street awash from an open hydrant, illustrating how 100-degree temperatures forced residents out of their stifling homes and into one another's company. A few experimental room air conditioners were produced in the 1930s, but they did not become commonplace until the 1950s. On the next page (top), South Philadelphia residents of Camac and McKean Streets sleep outdoors during a July 1934 heat wave. Even residents of relatively well-off Strawberry Mansion slept in Fairmount Park on hot summer nights. On the next page (below), a North Philadelphia family copes with too little heat in 1938. Like thousands of others throughout the city, this family had no central heating and relied on a coal- or coke-fired stove. In North Philadelphia below Poplar Street, a third of all families had no central heating as late as 1940.

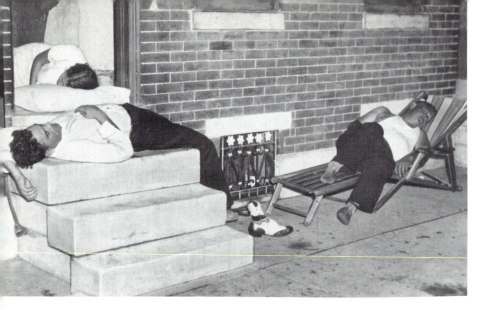

Residents of rowhouse neighborhoods drew strength from an elaborate network of ethnic and social organizations, ranging from churches and sporting clubs to political groups and labor unions. Neighborhood barbershops—like John Finney's at 809 South 13th Street—were important male community centers, but women were not welcome. The March 1939 photograph above was taken to illustrate the city's cramped polling places, of which this was one. Located between Catharine and Christian Streets near the heart of the city's oldest black neighborhood, Finney's Shaving Parlor was a well-established and prosperous-looking business as well as a social center. The ethnic press, another local institution, was especially important in keeping the city's smaller and more dispersed ethnic groups together. On the next page, Walter Serek delivers a copy of the local Czech paper to Mrs. Johanna Majerik of the 600 block of North Randolph Street—near the Fairmount Avenue center of Philadelphia's two-thousand-member Czech community—in 1938. German-born Philadelphians, by contrast, numbered over one hundred thousand. They were among the most prosperous of the city's ethnic communities. The 67th Annual Cannstater Volkfest took place in September 1940, and about five hundred members of the Volkfest Verein gathered at the Philadelphia Rifle Club at 8th and Tabor. The annual festival offered thousands an opportunity to listen to traditional German music and to watch or participate in traditional races and contests. As the photograph on page 13 indicates, this was very much a middle-class group, raising money for local charities and maintaining its ethnic traditions in spite of the approach of war between Germany and America.

The automobile transformed many of the city's older areas. Cars let middle-class residents abandon some districts for new suburbs; in other communities, the need to make room for cars might seal a neighborhood's doom. This photograph was part of a series meant to preserve a record of buildings torn down in the mid-1920s construction of the Delaware River (now Benjamin Franklin) Bridge. The houses on the 200 block of North Randolph Street (between Race and Vine, 5th and 6th) include a small wooden house, a reminder that this was one of Philadelphia's oldest intact neighborhoods. All the structures on this block— houses, several box factories, and a church—were lost in the bridge project. Hundreds of similar blocks just north of downtown survived bridge construction only to deteriorate gradually under the long-term impact of automobile traffic.

The unchanging physical appearance of the old streetcar suburbs during the 1920s and 1930s masked significant social change. Many of the earlier residents of these North and West Philadelphia districts outside the city's core moved farther outward into neighborhoods newly opened by the automobile in the 1920s. They were, in turn, replaced by more recent migrants to the city. These photographs depict North Philadelphia rowhouse neighborhoods west of Broad Street. The photograph above, taken about 1930, of the 2400 block of Bolton Street (between Jefferson and Oxford Streets) shows a block of substantial houses on the frontier of racial change at the end of the 1920s. To the south and east

was the growing black population of North Philadelphia. The area to the north and west, including the Glenwood Avenue industrial belt, was almost exclusively white. One of the most cohesive white communities was Strawberry Mansion, which extended roughly from 29th to 33rd Street and from Glenwood Avenue north to Lehigh. By the end of the 1920s, it was heavily populated by Jews of eastern European origin, many of whom were working people who had been able to move out of the old slums, but could not or would not move to better middle-class suburban areas. The photograph on the next page, taken by local amateur photographer Meyer Sherow, captured the kind of memories the Strawberry Mansion of the 1930s still evokes as a neighborhood where children could grow up both streetwise and

safe, an area definitely urban yet very much a community. Well-known local institutions, from synagogues to ice cream parlors, contributed to a community's identity. Cherry's Ice Cream Parlor was one such Strawberry Mansion institution. Located at the southeast corner of 33rd and Dauphin across from Fairmount Park, Cherry's was popular with everyone growing up in Strawberry Mansion in the 1930s. In fact, when the photograph on page 17 was taken in 1932, hundreds of families in the surrounding blocks were losing their homes to mortgage foreclosure as the Depression approached its nadir. Community life helped residents survive economic hardship and keep their neighborhood alive.

Rowhouse neighborhoods dating from the early twentieth century —neighborhoods newer than Strawberry Mansion—provided such semisuburban amenities as space and greenery. This 1941 scene of a child playing on an unidentified Philadelphia street depicts an uncrowded and fairly prosperous community—witness the white convertible. Similarly, the treelined view opposite, taken the same year near 48th and Locust, also conveys the more open, automobile-oriented flavor of that middle-class, mainly non-immigrant area. In fact, the Philadelphia *Record* (then one of the city's leading newspapers) meant the photograph to illustrate that on many such pleasant streets the traffic lights were practically invisible. Far to the north of City Hall, Feltonville, like much of West Philadelphia, was a product of the first quarter of the twentieth century. Located between Rising Sun Avenue and Tacony Creek, north of Courtland Street, the area was ethnically mixed, with substantial Jewish, German, and Irish populations. Though Feltonville depended on nearby industries, the plants—as in other newer communities—were isolated from the homes rather than interspersed among them. The photograph to the right, of the July 4, 1941, Feltonville parade, offers a view of a pleasant residential community built around parks rather than factories.

19

Philadelphia's suburban ring adjusted to the automobile during the 1920s and the 1930s. Automobile congestion in such ancient thoroughfares as Lancaster Avenue is visible in this mid-1930s photograph taken by the Pennsylvania Highway Department to document traffic-choked Ardmore. Shopping, commuting to work, and even socializing had become dependent upon the automobile in such middle- and upper-class communities. Almost ten years earlier, the opening of the Suburban Square shopping center had made Ardmore the site of one of the most significant landmarks in the development of the new metropolis. The shopping center, shown on page 22 in a dramatic nighttime photograph by Philip Wallace, was the creation of Frederick Dreher, a local department store architect. Dreher was convinced that stores could cut down on delivery expenses if people could park and shop in one place. By the time Strawbridge & Clothier opened the metropolitan area's first suburban department store in May 1930, Dreher had transformed the old Dixon estate into a modern shopping center, complete with expensive shops and parking for hundreds of cars. Though Suburban Square's size and compre-

hensive planning made it unique in this area, other automobile-oriented shopping centers were appearing here by the late 1920s, as the photograph of a new block of shops at Cooper and Broadway in Camden indicates (page 23, top). Placed in the middle of a traditional city, this center tried to accommodate pedestrians and automobiles simultaneously. Businessmen, planners, and officials struggled throughout the period to adapt to the new rules of the automobile city—not always successfully. In the photograph on the bottom of page 23, Isadore Friedman, who had a newsstand at 69th Street Station, checked parking meters outside the stores clustered near the Upper Darby shopping complex in July 1939. The merchants hired young entrepreneurs like Friedman to put pennies in expired meters so that their patrons would escape parking tickets.

At its outer fringes, greater Philadelphia shaded from suburbia into a rural landscape. Along the Pennsylvania Railroad's Main Line, wealthy suburbs seemed hardly connected to the city at all. The photograph by Philip Wallace (below) shows boys playing in front of spacious houses in Wayne, in August 1926. A. J. Drexel and George Child had developed Wayne as a railroad commuter suburb in the late nineteenth century. Wayne—about 16 miles from downtown—was consciously intended as a refuge from the city, but its well-to-do citizens were very much a part of the metropolitan community. In contrast, King of Prussia was a country village isolated from the city by virtue of its location several miles away from the Pennsylvania Railroad's commuter train service. The federal government's Bureau of Public Roads took the photograph opposite of the intersection of Routes 202 and 23 in the mid-1930s.

Different kinds of fringe areas—shantytowns and squatter settlements along the city's rivers and in its marshlands—housed hundreds of poor families with nowhere else to live. To the left, two mothers and their children are shown in Eastwick, in Southwest Philadelphia, in the 1930s. Crisscrossed by small creeks, canals, and dikes, Eastwick had been partially developed in the 1920s, when the area received its name, but the traditional truck farming area remained home to many squatters and poor farmers, including a substantial black community. Unlike Eastwick, the little shantytown along the Delaware River at Allegheny Avenue was located in the heart of an industrial area, just north of the Port Richmond Terminal of the Reading Railroad, and just south of an unhealthy complex of glue factories, brickyards, lumber mills, and tanneries. A Works Progress Administration (WPA) photographer captured the image on the opposite page, but it is unlikely that this waterfront village was a product of the Great Depression. Communities like this had existed for decades in other semirural parts of the city, their residents eking out a living from the soil or the river, until they were engulfed by the city or discovered by artists and social reformers.

Downtown Philadelphia had become a very special kind of neighborhood by 1930. Home to more than fifty thousand people, the area also served as the cultural, commercial, and entertainment center of the metropolitan region. The two panoramas of central Philadelphia illustrate the area's rapid growth during the 1920s. Above, a 1922 view from one of the new high-rise buildings on the south side of Rittenhouse Square looks east toward the emerging skyscraper downtown, with most of the tall buildings clustered in the rear of the scene, between City Hall and the equally distinctive mansard roof of the Bellevue-Stratford Hotel. By 1930, when the photograph to the right was taken, a more unified office tower district had been created west of Broad

along Chestnut and Walnut Streets as far as Rittenhouse Square. This aerial view shows all the key components of the classic downtown. On either side of City Hall were the two massive train stations— the Reading Terminal in the foreground and the Pennsylvania's Broad Street Station farther back. To the left of City Hall is John Wanamaker's. In the immediate foreground are the nineteenth-century commercial lofts north of Market Street, which still held many small factories and wholesale businesses, while in the background, broken by the industrial belt along the Schuylkill River, are the rowhouse blocks of South and West Philadelphia. The street-level view (on page 30) of South Broad Street looking north from Locust Street in 1931 captures a typical

busy downtown scene. One of the popular double-decker buses first introduced in 1923 makes its way between some of Philadelphia's oldest tall office buildings—several were almost three decades old by then. While such local landmarks as Horn & Hardhart and Conway's Tickets have disappeared, the view today remains much as it did then. By contrast, West Market Street was much different then, as this March 1941 view (on page 31) of trolleys lined up in a snowstorm indicates. Stretching along its northern side and precluding significant development was the Pennsylvania Railroad's notorious "Chinese Wall."

32

Rich and poor rubbed shoulders downtown, but they did not meet on equal terms; in many locations, middle-class values and appearances set the rules of appropriate social behavior. Even though the seven East Market Street department stores competed for the loyalties of all Philadelphians, they tried to cultivate an atmosphere of prosperity and respectability. Well-dressed patrons lunching in Lit Brothers' seventh-floor restaurant (at left) suggest the mass-produced luxury that the stores represented even in the middle of the Depression of the 1930s. Above, the 1937 scene in the spectacular concourse of 30th Street Station suggests a similar prosperity, but that may be because the Depression restricted intercity passenger rail traffic to the well-to-do. Built between 1928 and 1933, the neoclassical station—boasting restaurants and a cocktail lounge—was a reminder of the better days of the 1920s.

Many downtown districts featured people and services, entertainment and lifestyles, not found elsewhere in the metropolitan area. Particularly notable was the old Tenderloin, centered around 8th and Vine, which this late 1930s scene reveals to be a busy place. The Hotel Clover at 246 North 8th, with its 25-cent rooms, was typical of the neighborhood's flophouses, tattoo shops, pool halls, pawn shops, cheap taprooms, and penny arcades. Frequented by derelicts, soldiers and sailors on leave, and workers in loft industries, it was the kind of district that typically flourished on the edge of a thriving downtown. Only a block away was the closed world of Philadelphia's Chinatown, a tightly knit ethnic enclave of about a thousand people that had many legitimate enterprises but also had ancient ties to some of the Tenderloin's illegal enterprises. Two old men converse in front of the Far East Restaurant at 907 Race Street in the mid-1930s photograph on the opposite page. The restaurant—then the only local building decorated in a Chinese style—illustrates the transition of Chinatown from a place outsiders feared, because they associated it with opium dens and tong wars, to a neighborhood frequented because of its good restaurants and safe streets. There was yet another unusual downtown district—the ancient Dock Street Market. Since most activity here took place from 10 PM to 8 AM, this photograph (bottom, facing page) was probably taken in the early morning, and the workers were presumably reaching the end of their day's labor. From the delivery trucks, which began arriving before midnight, through the wholesale buyers of the early morning hours, to the retail marketers opening around sunrise, Dock Street ran on a uniquely contrary schedule. But like the Tenderloin and the nightclub area around Broad Street, Dock Street gave the downtown a 24-hour life that set it apart from the rest of the city.

The city's modernizing commercial life did not spell the end of older business practices. Street salesmen, common to both the downtown and to the adjacent immigrant neighborhoods, were regularly featured in newspaper articles on quaint reminders of a tradition stretching back to the colonial period; these photographs appeared in an April 1938 *Evening Bulletin* series. The flower seller (left) and the pretzel vendor (above) getting his shoes shined worked on Market Street east of City Hall. Though city officials repeatedly vowed to rid the main shopping district of vendors, the vendors persisted and actually increased in number during the Depression. They were tolerated largely because the goods and services they offered did not really compete with the modern downtown stores along Market Street. Streetside flower sellers, for example, proliferated around Easter, but were less noticeable the rest of the year. In the Jewish neighborhood below South Street, however, sidewalk merchants offered a much fuller array of products. A table of buttons is set up outside a kosher wine shop (page 38) and an apron salesman models his wares (page 39, top), both at 2nd Street and Fitzwater. Only a few blocks away, a clothing salesman incongruously pitches his goods in front of Finkelstein's Fish Market at 4th Street and Federal (page 39, bottom). These close-ups vividly reveal the intense personal give-and-take characteristic of curbside marketing. These scenes were not the consequence of the Depression. But by stalling economic development for a decade, the Depression allowed such traditional patterns of marketing to persist longer than might have been predicted in the booming 1920s.

Like many of the curb markets around the city, the strip along South 4th Street was one long shopping center, with curbside pushcarts complementing stores. What seemed quaintly disorganized to the outside observer was actually part of a complex economic system operating at the margins of mainstream economic institutions. 4th Street had been a center of Philadelphia Jewish life since the late nineteenth century. It continued, in the 1920s and 1930s, to serve a Jewish clientele, many of whom regularly returned from other sections of the city to shop here, as the sign on the corner store (above) offering to deliver Passover foods all over the city indicates. Signs amid the profusion of food announce such bargains as 45-cent shoes and 50-cent red flannel underwear in this mid-1930s WPA photograph. The caption originally accompanying the 1939 birdseye view of 4th Street (right) in the Philadelphia *Record* portrayed this as a scene of ethnic romanticism: "For more than 40 years the cries of the street merchants, the Babel of tongues of *hausfraus* of a dozen nationalities, the shouting of street urchins at the Fourth Street Market have provided the exciting overtones of the symphony of our city." But the photograph (top right) of figures carrying baskets of scrap on their backs, taken in South Philadelphia in April 1938, reminds us that long hours of hard work by people of all ages underlay the apparent charm and attractive prices of the ethnic economy.

41

The Knife
of the
Depression

There is a special poignance to the faces that stare out at us from the black-and-white photographs of the Great Depression. That we are touched by these images of poverty and struggle, dejection and survival, perhaps tells us as much about ourselves as it does about hard times in America in the 1930s. These are the recognizable poor, victims for whom we have special sympathy. Their lives echo the stories of our grandparents, their neighbors, and the people they knew and told us about. At least in recollection, the Great Depression was populated by individuals larger than life. Scraping by and making do with little, they discovered in the process their own inner resources or took strength from family and community. Other, shadowy figures, their spirits broken by failure, accent these accounts of survival. In truth, the people and events of the 1930s have taken on the quality of folklore. In the telling and retelling, they have become larger than life, contemporaries of Franklin Roosevelt and Lou Gehrig, characters worthy of *The Grapes of Wrath*.

The Great Depression owes its epic quality to the uncounted personal tragedies and acts of quiet heroism that marked the decade. No one could look far in a city as devastated as Philadelphia and avoid the fact of the Great Depression, but one might also be struck by how little—on the surface at least—the everyday lives of many citizens seemed to have changed. The city suffered in the 1930s, but many Philadelphians had already grown accustomed to hardship; some individuals even profited from the misfortune of the majority.

Significant continuities linked the Philadelphia of the 1930s with earlier decades. This had been and remained an immigrant city with an industrial economy. Neither fact promised easy lives. Even in good times, many jobs had been seasonal and uncertain. Luckier factory workers might hope to bring home full pay envelopes more frequently than their less fortunate peers, but—with irregular wages a regular feature of workers' lives—few in the industrial labor force could reasonably expect to avoid layoffs altogether. These economic insecurities meant that many fathers and husbands could not expect to support their families on their own. More than in any other American industrial city, wives and children were forced to take jobs to help make ends meet. In the late 1920s, the Bureau of Labor Statistics found Philadelphia families to average nearly two wage earners.

The city's industrial health had faltered noticeably as a temporary surge of war-related prosperity receded in the 1920s. It had been an artificial prosperity, willed by a government at war and unable to survive the return of peace. Layoffs at the Frankford Arsenal, Midvale Steel, and the

Unemployed veterans camping below
the Art Museum, 1932

Baldwin Locomotive Works decimated the workforce of some of the region's largest employers; the closing of the giant Cramp's Shipyard crippled the economy of Kensington, and the suspension of the government shipyard at Hog Island cost the jobs of more than twenty-five thousand workers. Military spending had not restored the city to its nineteenth-century preeminence as "workshop of the world"; nor had it helped reorient Philadelphia's industrial base toward emerging opportunities in mass production technologies. It had only masked the fundamental problems of a local economy tied to increasingly uncompetitive industrial strategies and outmoded products. New technologies, changes in styles, and the movement of local plants to sites in the suburbs or outside the region had rendered many workers superfluous. While some new industries—electrical appliances, electronics, and chemicals—had managed to gain a foothold or expand in the 1920s, such traditionally important sectors as the production of locomotives, leather goods, shipbuilding, and textiles in general and woolens in particular continued to shrink. From 1919 to 1927, Philadelphia manufacturing employment declined at almost twice the national rate.

In a survey made six months before the stock market crash of October 1929, the Bureau of Labor Statistics found one in ten wage earners in the city already unemployed. The same survey found that hardship fell unevenly across Philadelphia neighborhoods. Almost one in three workers was out of a job in some parts of densely populated South Philadelphia and in industrial districts in Kensington and Frankford. Sections of West Philadelphia and Chestnut Hill, on the other hand, experienced no unemployment. By the same token, factory and construction hands suffered disproportionately, while clerical workers and professionals enjoyed greater job security. The survey could surprise few in its findings that foreign-born Philadelphians were worse off than native-born whites, and that blacks were in the worst situation of all.

Few moments in history represent breaks with the past as dramatic and as overwhelming as the Great Depression. Unemployment soared as the city's economy collapsed. By the spring of 1932, four in ten of the city's workers were totally unemployed; another two in ten were reduced to part-time work. Some parts of the city—especially South Philadelphia and the industrial belt along the Delaware River—suffered disproportionately. So, too, some sectors of the economy were hurt more than others. Workers in the newer electrical and chemical industries were relatively more fortunate, but in some of the building trades eight in ten workers had been thrown out of work.

Firms continuing to operate did so with shortened hours and reduced wages. Some long established plants placed their skilled workers on indefinite furloughs. Others shut permanently. Suburban estates laid off their domestic servants and gardeners; hotels closed their dining rooms. Some of those who lost their jobs turned to peddling, more often hoping to survive than dreaming of entrepreneurial success. The mayor announced that twelve hundred Philadelphians had taken to the streets to sell apples. By 1933, per capita income in Pennsylvania had fallen to about half of its pre-crash level.

The Depression reached into the city's homes. Sheriff's sales turned thousands of homeowners into tenants, undermining Philadelphia's reputation as a city of owner-occupied homes. The problem of foreclosure was especially severe in the industrial districts along the river, in heavily immigrant South Philadelphia, and in the old streetcar neighborhoods. Because blacks were overwhelmingly tenants to begin with, foreclosure was the one problem of the Depression they avoided. New housing construction virtually ceased during the decade and the city's dramatic outward growth stopped, not to resume until after World War II. Dreams of homeownership, of moving into newly developing neighborhoods, had led more than one million Philadelphians to entrust over $800 million to the city's 3,400 savings and loan societies. By 1934, almost half of these societies had been wiped out, and the life savings of many were gone with them. Fifty banks folded as well, among them the large Bankers Trust, whose 100,000 depositors lost $35 million in deposits.

As the Depression deepened in the early 1930s, people tried to take care of their own, helping in the ways they had often aided the unfortunate. Neighborhood stores had generally offered credit, and many continued their policies, their owners sharing the misfortunes of customers in order to stay in business, and because they wanted to help. The city's police stations, traditionally a last resort for the homeless, offered the rudimentary hospitality of concrete floors to more than five hundred men a night by fall 1930. Ethnic communities and religious societies maintained, and in some cases expanded, the assistance they offered members and congregants. One count found eighty new breadlines and soup kitchens open in the city. A new city-wide organization, The Committee for Unemployment Relief, echoed earlier efforts to ride out hard times through private charity. The Committee raised $9 million in private contributions in 1930 and 1931, and spent the money sheltering homeless men, providing schoolchildren with breakfast, distributing coal and second-hand clothing, furnishing make-work jobs, and buying up to five dollars a week in groceries for impoverished families. But the old methods for dealing with short crises were inadequate to the long years of depression. The Committee, for example, provided milk only for young children who were sick. And, in any case, the Committee simply exhausted its funds and its prospects for raising more and disbanded in the spring of 1932 when the Depression was at its worst.

The Depression took its toll on family life. A 1934 housing survey found almost twenty-four thousand families doubling up and sharing quarters, sacrificing privacy to survive. The number of marriages in the city dropped by a third from 1929 to 1933, as couples postponed forming families because they could not afford to set up housekeeping or raise children. Live births plummeted by the same third. Divorces fell at an even greater rate, another sign of necessary compromise in personal lives. Even those who managed to maintain traditional patterns of family life were not unscathed. The Depression made its presence felt in children's lives, giving an especially hard edge to innocent childhood games, efforts to mimic and make sense of grown-up reality. One social worker found Philadelphia children "playing eviction" in the city's streets. She noted that sometimes they "played relief," but they preferred "eviction" because it had more action and they all knew how to play.

To be sure, many Philadelphians lived through the collapse of the financial system materially unscarred, retaining their jobs, their incomes, and their status. Professionals, business executives, teachers, social workers, clergymen, salespeople, and clerks fared much better than factory workers and laborers—though when the best-paid did lose their positions they tended to stay out of work for longer periods. Women workers had better luck keeping their jobs—or finding new ones—than men. Native white Americans suffered less than any other racial or ethnic group. The new automobile neighborhoods and older, prosperous communities like Chestnut Hill, Germantown, and the parts of West Philadelphia lying between Market Street and Baltimore Avenue were comparatively untouched. Though wages fell, the prices of many goods dropped even faster. The majority who held on to jobs had access to cheaper consumer goods, appliances, and supermarket foods. In the depths of the Depression, people still came to the Wissahickon Creek to feed the ducks at Valley Green. Even as congressional testimony revealed that some Philadelphians survived by gathering and eating dandelion greens, photographers recorded others on family picnics in Fairmount Park. Ironically, the depression decade was also a time when sports and games became increasingly popular. Softball and miniature golf, even contract bridge, occupied millions. But most popular of all was "Monopoly," a fantasy of real estate speculation in which chance and the roll of the dice decided who won. Many Philadelphians who played the game had actually been to the Boardwalk and Park Place in Atlantic City and had taken rides on the Reading.

The mixed photographic record is a reminder that experience was not uniform across the Depression. The crisis lasted the decade, but some years were more hopeful than others. New Deal programs helped stimulate a partial recovery in 1933, but that gave way to a renewed recession in 1937 and 1938. The same variation held on an individual level. Throughout the 1930s, most people who lost their jobs were able to find new ones, albeit at lower wages and sometimes after months of searching.

There is yet another reason for the variety of images that survive the Depression. So much of our memory of the decade derives from—and is confused by—radio and the movies, new technologies that came into their own during the decade. Movie attendance soared, offering an inexpensive time out. Even the blue laws bent to accommodate Hollywood when Philadelphians voted by referendum in 1935 to allow Sunday movies. Radios—many made in Philadelphia by Philco or Atwater Kent—entered millions of American homes, often on the installment plan. Both technologies were part of a vital, democratic popular culture. Both responded to the Depression in ways that were as complex as the event itself. But whether they presented nostalgia, fantasy, or even realism, both radio and the movies worked by offering an escape into the imagination. Both served to transform the economic catastrophe of the 1930s into a cultural phenomenon as well. It is ultimately on that level that an event as elemental in its force as the Great Depression remains in our memories.

The most vivid symbols of the Depression's early years were the camps of the jobless and the homeless, derisively called "Hoovervilles" in mock honor of an increasingly unpopular president. Philadelphia's largest camp —stretching along the Schuylkill River's east bank from the Art Museum to center city—was crowded with hundreds of men who had no place to go after the Shelter for Homeless Men at 18th and Hamilton closed, its funds having run out. Many of the shacks in these July 1932 scenes were built with materials from a nearby plumbing supply factory, which had been demolished the previous fall. Bill Berry adapted a more durable cinderblock railroad structure for his home shown below. Above, right, men bathe in the river, prepare food at makeshift ovens, and rest from their efforts to make money at odd jobs during the day. Unable to get long-term work, the men survived by gathering bricks and scrap iron for resale, and by begging and scavenging food. They also received food from sympathetic park guards. Though most of the men here are black, this Hooverville was also home to many whites, and to families as well as single men. Throughout the summer of 1932, the encampment was a constant reminder of the economic crisis and of the city's feeble response to it. But the approach of cold weather made other solutions imperative. In the fall, state funds reopened the shelter, and the park guards were ordered to destroy the shantytown. The photograph to the right, below, shows the destruction of one of the shacks still left in late October. The city's reopened shelter housed the Hooverville residents and about a thousand other men who had been sleeping in parks, police stations, and hallways, as they prepared for the worst winter of the Depression.

Unemployment ravaged Philadelphia's economy in the first years of the Depression. Opposite, homeless and out-of-work men—some doubtless from the nearby city shelter—congregate in Logan Circle in March 1933, as unemployment was at its peak. Unemployment was still high in January 1938, but by then a program of unemployment compensation provided some relief. Here, Philadelphians patiently line up outside the Armory at Broad and Callowhill on January 4, waiting to file claims on the first day of eligibility. Many are well dressed, reflecting not just the importance of the occasion, but also the fact that unemployment pay was available only to those who had worked recently, thus generally excluding the most destitute. While the compensation program was helpful, it did not solve the underlying problem of unemployment. On the next page, Harold Allertson and John Smith tour downtown Philadelphia looking for work in 1939. That same year, an *Inquirer* photographer captured the idle Cramp's Shipyard in Kensington (page 53). Cramp's had closed before the Depression, and —revived by World War II—would reopen a year after this photograph was taken. Yet even in 1940, the Depression persisted, and nearly 20 percent of the city's available labor force was unemployed or on relief projects.

The sign on the wagon reads:

WANTED
TWO GOOD JOBS
Willing Workers
Honest - Experienced
CALL STE-6050

Hunger stalked thousands of Philadelphia families during the Depression. There were few reported deaths from starvation, but malnutrition and undernourishment were common. According to one 1936 report, children and parents in forty-eight thousand Philadelphia families were going to bed hungry. That seventy-one thousand families the same year were making do with insufficient food, clothing, or heat indicated that hardcore distress survived the mid-1930s introduction of government relief programs. Here, in a ritual of charity that predated the Depression, a mother and her son carry home free vegetables distributed to the needy at Ritner and Swanson Streets in South Philadelphia in July 1938. To the right (top), the House family of 12th and Fairmount have their main meal of the day in August 1939. William House had worked for Strawbridge & Clothier for nine years, but now received $14.80 per week in relief to care for his family of six. The $6-per-week rental for a two-room apartment left enough for the family to survive, but hardly anything for emergencies or entertainment. The photograph below —illustrating an October 1941 report published in the *Inquirer* asserting that one hundred and sixty thousand undernourished children attended the city's schools—shows Mrs. Emma Bright serving lunch to her South Philadelphia family. Lunch for her four small children consisted of soup, the mainstay of the family's diet—and all that a Mother's Assistance check of $58 per month ordinarily allowed for.

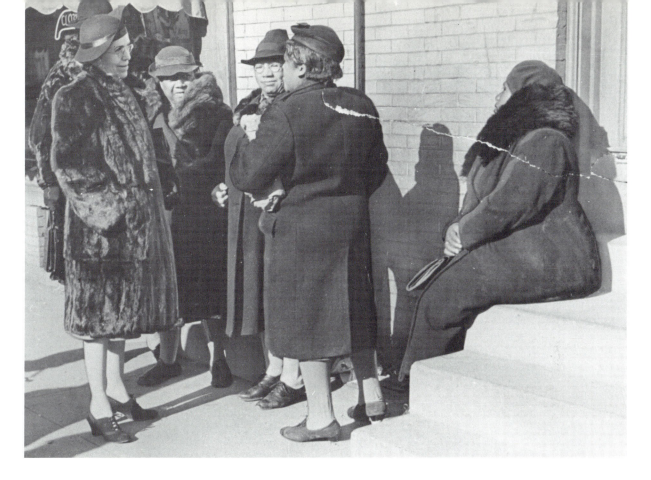

Even for many people with jobs, the 1930s were hardly a time of prosperity. Problems of short hours, reduced wages, and intermittent layoffs predated the 1930s but grew more severe during the Depression. The men waiting for a freighter to dock along the Delaware River, in the photograph (opposite page) taken in 1937 for the WPA's Pennsylvania Art Project, remind us of the way casual laborers had to hope for work on a day-to-day basis. Similarly, the December 1939 photograph above shows what some called the "slave mart" for domestic servants at 7th and Snyder in South Philadelphia. Here, women—mostly black—came every day in the hope of being hired by local housewives. As the *Record* reported, women might ask 20 cents an hour for their work and might be offered 15 cents in nego-tiating their daily terms. Elsewhere in the city similar hiring practices had become regularized in other casual labor industries. The men depicted on the next page were probably suffering more directly from the Depression. These pictures, taken along Market Street in November 1937, reveal street vendors who look like the white-collar and professional men who had been reduced to selling goods on the street or door-to-door. This was often the last financial resort for those with no physical or industrial skills.

Even in the very depths of the Depression, the city's economy was ravaged but not destroyed; more people in the labor force had jobs than didn't. Philadelphia's industrial diversity cushioned the impact of the slump, making it less severe here than it was in one-industry cities dependent on steel or coal. Devastated industries like textiles still employed tens of thousands of workers, and a wide variety of companies continued to provide such basic necessities as food, fuel, and transportation. Photographers for the WPA and the Farm Security Administration (FSA) in the mid-1930s documented more Philadelphians working than unemployed. Here, Paul Vanderbilt of the FSA depicted two workmen in a coalyard near the Schuylkill above South Street in spring 1936. When a local WPA photographer recorded women in the automated packaging department of the Pennsylvania Sugar Company about 1936 (next page, top), the plant at Delaware and Shackamaxon in Kensington employed 1,100 workers and produced about 250 railroad carloads of Quaker Sugar every day. The company had its own wharf where steamers from the Caribbean and the Pacific unloaded raw sugar. Philadelphia's position as the second-largest sugar refinery center in the world meant that the city's economy profited from the drastic fall in foreign produce prices brought on by the Depression. The local textile industry, by contrast, was especially hard hit, but there were still more than forty thousand workers employed in textiles at the end of the decade, and textiles and clothing together remained the region's largest industrial sector. The survival of part of the city's once-dominant industry is documented at the bottom of the next page. LaFrance Industries, located at Orthodox and Large Streets in Frankford, employed almost six hundred workers in the manufacture of plush upholstery fabrics. Like the image of the coalyard workmen, it is a good example of contemporary photographic efforts to emphasize the dignity of work and the working man. The photograph at the top of page 61 puts more emphasis on the complexity of modern machinery, but it also depicts work which went on throughout the Depression— in this case public transportation. Shown here in the late 1930s, this is the Race Street Tower control station of the Reading Railroad. The last photograph, at the bottom of page 61, is a less heroic depiction of Philadelphia's continuing tradition of metal craftsmanship. It was taken in the fall of 1939 in the Budd Company machine shop at 24th and Hunting Park Avenue. Many of these men had been recently recalled to work after a layoff and were checking over their tools and machines. The photograph thus captures both the persistence of skills and the uncertainty of employment that characterized the decade.

Philadelphia's position as a center of technologically advanced industry throughout the 1930s also lessened the impact of the Depression. Pharmaceuticals—as this photograph of Sharp and Dohme's laboratory at Broad and Wallace suggests—were a case in point. Sharp and Dohme, which had come to Philadelphia in 1929 as a result of a merger with an older local company, was one of the nation's leading drug manufacturers, employing about a thousand workers in its city plant and another several hundred at a biological laboratory in Glenolden, Delaware County. This WPA photograph emphasizes the technological complexity of flasks, valves, and containers, as well as the lighted face of the scientist or technician, apparently in an attempt to convey an image of modern science at work. The Erecting Camera Department of the Lanston Monotype Manufacturing Company around 1936 represents another of the city's technical industries (top of facing page). Founded in 1892 by the inventor of the monotype machine, Lanston had become one of the nation's major manufacturers of such specialized publishing equipment as this huge commercial camera. Even in the depths of the Depression, the company still employed about six hundred workers in its plant at 24th and Locust when this photograph was taken. The broad industry of which Lanston was a part—printing and publishing—employed almost twenty-two thousand Philadelphians at the end of the 1930s. Below, right, another photograph depicts and celebrates old-fashioned craft work in the even newer radio industry. With RCA in Camden and Philco and (until 1936) Atwater Kent in Philadelphia, the area was one of the national centers of radio production. Despite the

Depression, Philco and Atwater Kent together employed more than six thousand industrial workers in 1933. Throughout the decade, the national demand for radios kept the industry growing. Most industry workers were young and many were women, largely because radio manufacture used modern mass-production methods and required relatively little physical labor. However, specialized operations were often exceptions. This scene shows a cabinet repairman at RCA in Camden in 1937 cutting away some veneer damaged during the assembly of the radio. Social-reformer–photographer Lewis Hine, who was in Philadelphia for the WPA's National Research Project, took this picture. Most of the cabinetworkers in the radio industry had been recruited from the cabinet and furniture trades, and were generally older Italian men. They kept traditional work skills alive in one of the area's most important new industries.

Just as most people continued to work during the Depression, so most continued to play. Even in the face of limited means, it was not uncommon for Philadelphians to put aside some time and money to enjoy themselves. If anything, the Depression strengthened old-fashioned family outings and local diversions like those pictured here, simply because so many Philadelphians lacked the money to do much else. One typical inexpensive and popular outing was an expedition to Boulevard Pools, one of the largest of the city's private outdoor pools, which competed successfully with the public bathing beaches at Pleasant Hill in Torresdale and at League Island. Shown above are some of the six thousand bathers who visited Boulevard Pools on June 30, 1935. For many city dwellers, an expedition to Boulevard Pools at Princeton and Tyson Streets in the Northeast brought many of the attractions of the Jersey shore or a trip to the country within easy commuting distance. Baseball also felt few adverse effects from the Depression as the crowd, on the facing page, at the first Ladies' Day of the 1938 season at Shibe Park, traditional home of the American League Athletics, suggests. With both Shibe Park and the Phillies' pre-1938 home, Baker Bowl, on mass transit lines in North Philadelphia, and good seats available for under a dollar, baseball remained within the means of most. In sharp contrast to later years, however, the crowd shown here was virtually all white, even if disproportionately female. The city had its own very good black teams, such as the Philadelphia Stars, with black followings. But in 1938 few commented openly on the irony of segregated major league ball played in increasingly black Philadelphia before white crowds.

Informal family outings in city parks remained within the means of most. Below, a Philadelphia *Record* photographer captured the scene for a June 1937 article complaining about the lack of comfort stations in Fairmount Park. This group of Strawberry Mansion residents picnicking in the East Park adjoining their neighborhood suggests how gatherings of family and friends made the Park so important to Philadelphians. The view at Valley Green to the right, documented by amateur photographer Meyer Sherow in the late 1930s, shows one of the most popular and inexpensive of all local pastimes, feeding the ducks that gathered there on summer days. The Valley Green Inn had been restored and refurbished in 1936 and 1937 as part of the ongoing process—dating from the early 1920s—of transforming the Wissahickon Valley into a recreational area. The early springtime scene, to the right, below, indicates the popularity of the Wissahickon with rowers, canoeists, swimmers, and fishermen. These images portray another side of the 1930s—not poverty or politics, but the effort to cope, and to escape the Depression with simple pleasures.

The Mummers' parade was an important symbol of the continuity of working-class traditions through the crisis of the Depression. Though the neighborhoods which sustained the parade were among those hardest hit by the Depression, the show went on. Above, some of the thousands lining the streets to see the parade resorted to time-honored methods of getting the best view. The caption accompanying this photograph in the Philadelphia *Record* noted that the police had ordered that no one should stand on a basket to watch the parade, quizzically adding, "Izzat so?" Five fancy clubs, six comic clubs, and eighteen string bands participated in the 1938 parade. Following their custom, the comic clubs poked fun at politicians and celebrated the city at the same time. To the right, the Murray Comic Club depicts the new airport, which Mayor S. Davis Wilson had decided to name after himself. The first twenty Murray paraders had appeared in long underwear carrying telescopes—a reference to City Council's perennial search for a solution to the Gas Works crisis.

Children growing up in the city's neighborhoods amused themselves much as their parents had, adapting traditional games to the urban landscape. An April 1938 *Bulletin* feature recorded the springtime start of baseball and jump rope (opposite page), games typically played even in Philadelphia's narrowest streets. The third photograph, on the right, was another in the June 1937 *Record* series documenting the lack of toilet facilities in the city's parks—in this case Passyunk Square. Once more, a photograph of an odd subject preserved an interesting slice of life—two boys playing cards while another watched, and all three in dress shirts with at least one wearing a tie!

Despite the persistent economic crisis, the 1930s witnessed important innovations in popular culture and entertainment. Among them was the opening of the world's first drive-in movie theater in June 1933, on Admiral Wilson Boulevard in Camden, just west of the old Airport Circle. Built in secrecy in cooperation with nearby RCA, the Drive-In—which was its name from the start—had a capacity of four hundred cars in seven inclined rows (opposite page). The promoter claimed that drive-ins would be especially attractive to families with small loud children,

the old and infirm, and smokers. Success was not immediate, however; the drive-in boom really did not come until after the war. The next scene, above, captures a genuine phenomenon of the late 1930s —jitterbugs dancing the boogie-woogie to "swing." Philadelphia was caught up in the swing music craze that swept the country in 1937 and 1938. A record player and a few platters by such band-leaders as Benny Goodman, Artie Shaw, or Tommy Dorsey could turn almost any open space into a dance floor. In this 1938 Philadelphia *Record* photograph, Kitty Gaston, Phil Alomar, Molly Dorfman, and Max Wolfson show off their steps at a jitterbug contest at 124 Market Street. Though live

concerts attracted thousands, it was the record player that made dances like this affordable to young people in the 1930s, and broadened the audience for hot jazz and swing music beyond New York. A night at a Philadelphia jitterbug dance could cost as little as the 10-cent minimum and usually stayed under a half-dollar. Though more a product of the continuing Depression than the drive-in, the swing craze was just as much a preview of the mass popular culture that flowered so exuberantly after World War II.

Family Album, 1920s and 1930s

A snapshot of four women taken in the early 1920s on the 2300 block of Dickinson Street. Left to right are Lena Moran, her daughter Yetta, a neighbor, and another daughter, Sadie. Notice the Model T Ford and the child across the street cleaning the sidewalk.

David Kendis, age seven, was coming home from school one day in 1923 when his mother spotted a man with a delivery wagon. She lifted her son on to the pony's back and ran to get her camera. The photo was taken in the Strawberry Mansion section of the city near 2600 North 32nd Street.

A Kendis family picnic in Fairmount Park in the summer of 1923. One can almost hear the family photographer urging the group to look at the camera and to crowd together. The children are carefully arranged in the front with the grandmother on the left. David Kendis, who preserved this photograph, is the third child on the left. His father, Maurice Kendis—on the right—was also known as Tommy Stagg during his boxing days early in the century.

Three recent immigrants to Philadelphia relax in the summer of 1926 on the Schuylkill near the Strawberry Mansion Bridge. John Hofferberger arrived from Leipzig, Germany in 1923; Michael Weadislav Grabowski came in the same year from Kolomea, Poland; Josephine Maier Grabowski arrived from Vienna, Austria, also in 1923. Although the big influx of immigrants into the city had ceased by the 1920s and 1930s, Philadelphia was still a haven for those fleeing Europe between the wars.

The Wagner family in the mid-1920s in the backyard of their house at 2856 East Pacific Street near the intersection of Richmond and Venango, a section of the city destroyed in the 1960s by the construction of Interstate 95. This house, like many in the neighborhood, had sheds, coops, and stables. A garden is visible to the left. Sam Wagner and his wife Amelia are standing. On the bench are Fred (holding one of his father's pigeons), Millie, and Kay.

Marjorie Beers Poole cooling off during the summer of 1923 at 48th and Aspen Streets.

9/11/27

G.

A Dodge Roadster and its proud owner, Garrett Magens, in 1927. The top came down and it had a rumble seat. Note the wooden spokes and the running board. The windshield wiper was worked by hand and there was no heater. Passengers used lap robes in the winter. A new car like this cost about $800 in 1927.

Vacations were regular opportunities for family photography. This 1925 photograph records members of Philadelphia's Bowser family—Viola and her brothers John and Robert—relaxing on the beach in Ocean City, New Jersey. This photograph does not reveal the racial (and religious) segregation that prevailed at much of the Jersey shore.

Three young women, dressed a little like flappers, relax in the backyard of a house in the 2800 block of Emerald Street some time in the late 1920s. Two are teachers and the other a secretary, all from the nearby Powers School. Note the dog, a favorite subject for family photographers.

Lila and Constance Gould in their dress-up clothes in the summer of 1931 in front of their house at 5350 Locust Street. Lila, on the left, graduated from West Philadelphia High School in February 1940 and entered Temple University. She left college after two years to get married but returned to Temple more than forty years later to graduate in 1984. Her sister graduated from Temple in 1948.

A summer day on Market Street in the early 1930s. The well-dressed gentleman in the foreground is Clarence Mason, a Ford automobile salesman who would soon lose his job, forcing his family to accept welfare. Notice the hats on both men and women. This picture was probably taken by a professional photographer who took photos of selected people on the street and then tried to sell them prints.

Many people proudly took photographs of their businesses as well as of their cars and children. This is the Cadillac Delicatessen and Restaurant at 1940 Green Street, photographed in September 1931, with the proprietor, Isidor Plumer, standing among his wares. The deli served several Temple University professional schools, which were then in the area. The Dental School was at 18th and Buttonwood; the Medical School and Optometry School in the 1800 block of Spring Garden. The well-dressed students on the left eating a quick lunch are from one of these schools.

This mid-1930s photograph by Meyer Sherow shows his son, Marvin, enjoying a milkshake in the family's Strawberry Mansion kitchen while a cousin looks on.

A family record of children coming of age might include their early commercial transactions. Here, Marvin Sherow buys water ices from a cart in Strawberry Mansion in the mid-1930s.

Pat Worthington in front and her sister Nancy, near their 210 Ruscomb Street home, probably in the summer of 1933. Many Philadelphia family albums seem to have at least one photograph of a child on a pony. The presence of a pony—and such pictures—were often features of area birthday parties.

Philadelphians have always made good use of the stoops and the streets in front of their houses. Here a group of young men are playing pinochle on the sidewalk at 39th and Pennsgrove on a summer Sunday afternoon in 1934. Samuel Salzman who preserved the photo, is facing the camera to the right. His brother Max is standing to the right "watching with pride the fact he taught me how to play pinochle." The photographer was Max Waxman, the brother of Lillian Comroe, the young woman with her son in her arms looking at the camera.

Rose LoCicero at her confirmation May 5, 1935, at the Epiphany Church, 1121 Jackson Street. Rose was one of nine children of Salvatore and Santa LoCicero, who lived at 1937 South 12th Street. Mrs. LoCicero designed and made the dress. The photograph appears to have been taken by a professional photographer. It is carefully posed with flowers, rosary, and prayer book. Photographs of such symbolic occasions became treasured keepsakes.

The New Deal City

Old certainties gave way as the Depression tightened its grip. The long-standing American expectation that individuals were responsible for their own destinies—a value sometimes challenged in the past but never abandoned—was itself a victim of the unprecedented hard times. Franklin Delano Roosevelt assumed the presidency in 1933 promising a New Deal. He was sometimes hesitant and rarely consistent, but gradually his administration created an activist federal government, committed to intervening in the nation's economic life to promote its goals of a living wage and a decent home for all Americans. In part because of the New Deal, but often for other reasons as well, the 1930s witnessed an extraordinary transformation of the nation's political culture. By the mid-1930s, demonstrations, manifestoes, and protests by political and economic activists—including organized labor, peace groups, ethnic societies, and political radicals—were a regular feature of life in communities like Philadelphia.

Traditional ideals and practices did not recede easily in Philadelphia. In the early 1930s, the city's Republican administration was consistently opposed to governmental job, housing, and relief efforts. Indeed, State Senator George Woodward, heir to the family fortune that developed Chestnut Hill, was so hostile to federal projects that he used his own money to create jobs for the unemployed. Woodward's project turned part of Cresheim Valley into an addition to Fairmount Park.

But local opposition to activist government was rarely so constructive. Taking office in January 1932, Mayor J. Hampton Moore announced that there was no depression, and noted that only the lazy and thriftless were in trouble. Rather than continue the city government's limited efforts to extend assistance to the needy, Moore retrenched, firing thirty-five hundred city workers, cutting the pay of others, instituting unpaid vacations for police and firemen, and suspending new municipal construction to help balance the budget. Responding to the doubling-up of thousands of Philadelphia families in crowded housing and the presence of thousands of others in dilapidated structures, the mayor noted that "people are merely living within their means." Moore's term as mayor coincided with the worst of the Depression, but over those four years the city did not contribute a cent to relief. Local officials could have been more sensitive to the unemployed, but it is unlikely that they could have handled the problem with city dollars. Falling tax revenues from pinched property owners meant that the city was hard-pressed to pay its ordinary bills. Ultimately, Philadelphia had to mortgage the Philadelphia Gas Works (PGW)—the municipally owned gas company—to fund its Depression-era expenses.

Women of the WPA Sewing Project,
1941

Given the inaction of local government, it is not surprising that some Philadelphians took matters into their own hands. Stalked by starvation, some turned to begging, others to picking through garbage, and yet others to theft. A congressional witness testified about families who went along the Delaware River docks, picking up vegetables that fell from wagons. The hungry stole milk and groceries from doorsteps, and in cold weather the unemployed pillaged vacant houses for firewood. But there was also collective action, for the Great Depression politicized the American people as few other events had. Union organizers and political radicals found receptive audiences for their messages of direct action among the city's unemployed. Hosiery and carpet weavers organized an Unemployed Citizens League in May 1932. Like similar groups in other cities, the league returned furniture and belongings to homes from which it had been removed by eviction; they turned on utilities disconnected when bills went unpaid. In August 1932, a mass march of the unemployed brought their anguished plea to City Hall. Unmoved, Mayor Moore ordered the police to disperse the marchers, precipitating the battle of Reyburn Plaza when the police tried to break up a rally of the unemployed. This violence at the very doors of City Hall brought Philadelphia unwelcome national notoriety.

Unemployed Philadelphians fared better in Harrisburg. Taking office in 1931, reform governor Gifford Pinchot believed that the Pennsylvania Constitution forbade state expenditures for unemployment relief. But when the state Supreme Court ruled, in April 1932, that such spending was constitutional, Pinchot committed the government to relieve the suffering of the unemployed. Soon after the disastrous confrontation in the shadows of City Hall, Pinchot established a Philadelphia County relief board to funnel state money into the city. By April 1935, the state was supporting one hundred and six thousand Philadelphia families on emergency relief. Pinchot actually organized a "little new deal," making Pennsylvania's efforts to provide relief and jobs a model for other states. George Earle, his Democratic successor in 1935, was unable to convince Senate conservatives to continue funding for relief until hunger marchers descended on the state capitol in the spring and summer of 1936.

Ultimately, the state government—like individual effort or private charity—proved no match for the Great Depression. Only the federal government had the resources to address the massive dislocations of the era—and those resources were applied only tentatively. The New Deal's first efforts barely reached Philadelphia because the city government refused to cooperate with federal authorities. The city's Republican politicians feared aid from a Democratic administration in Washington might disrupt the voter loyalties on which their entrenched political machine depended. Since the late nineteenth century, the votes of the poor, the city's newer immigrants, and its blacks had kept Philadelphia's Republicans in power. These groups had provided the margin of victory for Herbert Hoover's election-day triumph over FDR in the city. Even with only minimal direct federal intervention in the city, political allegiances in Philadelphia shifted. Blacks, Jews, and workers in general, mirroring national trends, abandoned the Republican Party. When Democrat S. Davis Wilson, running as a Republican, won the November 1935 mayoral election, the New Deal finally arrived in Philadelphia. Roosevelt carried the city by an overwhelming majority in 1936.

New Deal programs—the Works Progress Administration, the Civilian Conservation Corps, and the National Youth Administration—permanently altered the face of the city. Federally funded laborers graded runways for the new international airport and overhauled the water filtration plants. They landscaped the Philadelphia Zoo, installed period rooms at the Museum of Art, built Sullivan Hall as a library for Temple University, and laid out neighborhood playgrounds. Unemployed clothing workers sewed uniforms in federal factories for the postal service, and the WPA hired carpenters and furniture makers to refurbish chairs and desks for more than one hundred Philadelphia public schools. The government financed model housing projects near Juniata Park and at Hill Creek in the earlier years of the New Deal, and turned to less successful slum clearance and low-income housing as the 1940s began.

The park system was a special beneficiary of federal largesse. New guardhouses appeared in Cobbs Creek Park; Harper Meadow, a twenty-acre tract at the city's northwestern boundary, was filled in and landscaped as a picnic and recreation spot; new roads, trails, and walls were built throughout the park and older ones were reconstructed. At the peak of WPA activity in the summer of 1936, more than forty-seven thousand Philadelphians worked for the federal agency. Their jobs helped them survive the Depression; their work can still be seen in many areas of the city.

Federal programs in Philadelphia rearranged more than the natural landscape and built with more than bricks and mortar. The Treasury Department commissioned artists to paint murals of American life in the Customs House and local post offices, democratizing original art and placing it within the everyday experiences of ordinary Philadelphians. The WPA organized orchestras, paying musicians to give concerts in community centers. The Federal Writers Project hired hundreds of authors, photographers, and typists to produce *Philadelphia: A Guide to the Nation's Birthplace*, the local volume in the American Guide Series, in 1937. Federally funded recreation programs taught sports to the young, and literacy and citizenship classes brought English-language skills and American values to older immigrants. None of these programs ended the Depression, but all provided jobs and incomes. Most built a sense of common purpose among their participants; many promoted a vision of a just and democratic America.

The New Deal brought many outsiders closer to the mainstream of American life. The federal government effectively enfranchised the labor movement, giving workers the right to organize and bargain collectively through both the National Industrial Recovery Act (NIRA) of 1933 (struck down as unconstitutional in 1935) and the National Labor Relations Act (NLRA) of 1935. The legislation had an enormous impact in Philadelphia, where a strongly anti-union and open-shop environment had crushed union activity in the 1920s. The NIRA ushered in a year of organizing strikes—many of them successful—among textile workers, painters and paperhangers, pocketbook makers, necktie workers, cab drivers, and actors. When the NLRA endorsed the organization of less skilled industrial workers, the new Congress of Industrial Organization (CIO) unleashed a nationwide wave of sit-down strikes in 1937. These reached into Philadelphia when eighteen hundred workers won a seven-week strike against the Electric Storage Battery Company and twenty-three hundred workers successfully struck Apex Hosiery.

The New Deal shifted other loyalties as well. Many newcomers in Philadelphia's ethnic and racial communities found themselves torn between traditional identification with their groups and an increasingly strong allegiance to a newly powerful and benevolent state. In the industrial, immigrant, and black neighborhoods of cities like Philadelphia, the New Deal represented more than an effort to address economic collapse; it opened the possibilities of a fuller American citizenship. For these diverse communities which had long existed on the fringe of American life, the New Deal joined the American Revolution in the national pantheon.

The federal programs of the 1930s enabled hundreds of thousands of Philadelphians to weather the most severe economic catastrophe in the history of the nation. Though intended to be temporary, to tide Americans through a hard time, these federal initiatives had far-reaching consequences. They rebuilt many of Philadelphia's roads and bridges, redistributed political power locally, and signaled a new—though ultimately uncertain—public commitment to the maintenance of minimum standards in housing and income. Yet with all these successes, the New Deal did not end the Depression. Prosperity returned to Philadelphia—and to the rest of industrial America— when war broke out in Europe and military contracts rescued the regional economy.

For all the transforming power of Depression and New Deal, older themes persisted through the period, impressing their shapes on the culture and politics of the decade. As news of a rearming Europe reached Philadelphia, ethnic loyalties assumed new significance. Foreign-language papers carried news of different homelands, the Bund recruited among German-Americans, and local Jews opened their homes to a handful of fortunate refugees. By the end of the 1930s, international conflict had replaced the domestic economic crisis at the center of American concerns, drawing Philadelphians out of Depression and into war.

The 1920s politics of quiescence gave way to the agitated politics of the Depression. Less than six months after the Wall Street crash, Philadelphia's Communist Party—its public support growing in the wake of economic collapse—organized a series of protests against unemployment, including the February 1930 demonstration on the north side of City Hall shown above. Though the Communist Party was then extremely weak and isolated, its meetings and marches attracted significant attention; large crowds gathered whenever several hundred activists marched downtown. While the police occasionally broke up these early meetings, especially if marchers attempted

to enter City Hall *en masse*, they were under orders to avoid violence for fear of creating martyrs. While ignoring the Communists and the unemployed, the city's conservative administration paid close attention to taxpayer protests. Pictured to the right, above, is a December 1931 march against real estate tax increases that illustrates how the Depression stimulated activism across the social and political spectrum. By then, the economic crisis had eroded the city government's ability to collect enough revenue to maintain city services. Leaders of neighborhood business groups led marchers downtown from 24th and Ridge, deliberately following the route taken by 1905

protesters fighting the corrupt gas works. Pressure like this forced City Council to approve firing city workers rather than raising taxes. Right, the march of several thousand Philadelphia Jews stepping off at 5th and Washington on May 10, 1933 illustrates other aspects of the 1930s crisis that reached Philadelphia. The parade protesting anti-Semitic actions of Germany's new Nazi government ended at City Hall, where marchers denounced the Hitler regime. Like the protests of the Left and the Right, such open concern about events abroad would be a continuing feature of the decade.

The most dramatic incident of the unemployment crisis of the early 1930s was the August 25, 1932, "Battle of Reyburn Plaza." Two years of demonstrations by the unemployed had led by mid-1932 to the creation of the Unemployed Councils and Leagues. With the collapse in June of private charitable efforts—and no relief available from public agencies—these organizations determined to march on the City Council. A crowd of about fifteen hundred—watched by fifty policemen and park guards —stopped to hear speeches on the south side of Reyburn Plaza just north of City Hall, violating police orders that they keep moving. The police then waded into the crowd with their riot sticks (above), arrest-

ing ten marchers and knocking down more than a dozen in clearing the plaza. John Parks, head of the Unemployed Councils, was injured and arrested in the melee, and is shown (at the right) being led away. Ironically, as the crowd was fighting the police outside, its representatives had been granted permission to address City Council, which they asked for public relief. The city refused, and Mayor J. Hampton Moore noted that there were "few, if any, taxpayers or American Legion veterans in the nondescript crew" on Reyburn Plaza. John Parks was convicted of rioting, but continued to agitate on behalf of the unemployed. Very much a symbol of his time, Parks was later one of the first American volunteers to fight against Franco in Spain, and he was killed there late in 1937.

New Deal job relief programs began to transform the physical face of the metropolitan area in late 1933. The Civil Works Administration—or CWA—began first, hiring its first local employees in December 1933 and maintaining about twenty-five thousand people on its payroll by March 1934. Among the more visible CWA projects was the improvement of the Philadelphia Zoo. More than four hundred men refurbished buildings, painted cages and fences, built moats and even remodeled the buffalo house. Above, workmen in January 1934 repave the roadway in front of the zoo's administration building, John Penn's eighteenth-century mansion. Pennsylvania's Local Works Division succeeded the CWA in April 1934; the national Works Progress Administration followed in April 1935. Despite

initial city government resistance, thirty thousand Philadelphians were at work on WPA projects by August. But the city's reluctance to fund projects finally led the WPA to send eligible city workers to projects in more cooperative suburban jurisdictions. On the next page, WPA workers fill the Reading Company yard at 3rd and Berks in December 1935. The workers, who traveled daily to state highway projects in Bucks County, were protesting that they had not been paid for several weeks. But the WPA was no solution to the area's unemployment problem. At its peak in mid-1936, it employed about forty-eight thousand workers, less than one-third of the city's unemployed. Thereafter, WPA employment in Philadelphia was steadily reduced to about twenty thousand by the start of

1939, and pay scales were cut to subsistence relief levels. New Deal agencies nevertheless continued to play an important role in the physical rehabilitation of the city right up to the start of the war. The National Youth Administration (NYA), which aided high school and college students and provided jobs for young people, was particularly popular. Shown below on the next page, integrated NYA work crews plant shrubs near Greenland Mansion in Fairmount Park in September 1939. The New Deal left the Philadelphia area a tangible legacy of hundreds of new and rebuilt parks, roads, bridges, waterways, and public buildings.

The New Deal had only a minimal impact on Philadelphia's serious housing problem. Disagreements between the Democratic administration in Washington and local Republicans delayed most public housing construction until the end of the decade, despite the fact that a 1939 survey found eighty thousand substandard houses in the city. Only the Carl Mackley Houses and the Hill Creek project had been opened by then. The Hosiery Workers Union used a loan from the Public Works Administration to build the Mackley Houses, at M and Bristol Streets in Juniata Park, in 1934. Here, architect Oscar Stonorov's strikingly modern design featured porch balconies, narrow sunlit buildings, and walls of glazed terra-cotta tiles. Set among three acres of open space planted in lawns and gardens, the four apartment buildings also boasted a cooperative food store, a pool, and other community facilities. Later public housing projects lacked the full range of amenities and the excitement of innovation which characterized the Mackley project, but contained similar community buildings and open spaces. Hill Creek—also funded with Public Works Administration funds—opened in 1938 at Adams and Rising Sun Avenues. Every Hill Creek apartment had a combined kitchen and dining room, equipped with a three-burner electric stove, double sink, and electric ice-box. The photograph at the right was probably taken in one of the five-room apartments, which rented for about $34 per month. Though an obviously posed and idealized family setting, the scene conveys the comfortable yet definitely working-class standard of living that New Deal housing projects were designed to provide.

By late 1941, the four-year-old Philadelphia Housing Authority had used federal loans to open or start construction on about three thousand units in three projects— Richard Allen and James Weldon Johnson Homes in North Philadelphia and Tasker Homes in South Philadelphia. Public housing initially improved the lot of its residents, but it would eventually prove inadequate as a solution to the housing problem. These photographs document the early 1941 move of the Vincent Suarez family from a three-room bandbox house near 3rd and Poplar to the newly opened Tasker Homes. The original one-bedroom house was impossibly crowded for a family with three young children. Mrs. Suarez bathed her baby in a tin washtub (top); her oldest child slept on a studio couch (middle). The family did its bathing and washing in the cramped coal stove-heated kitchen (bottom). In its new home, the family had two bedrooms, modern gas and electric appliances, and access to modern community laundries. The image, on the right, of Mrs. Suarez standing proudly before her new home with her children suggests that women and children derived the greatest benefit from the limited public housing built in Philadelphia by the New Deal.

The federal government also funded social service and training programs, providing jobs to the unemployed and services to families scraping along on relief payments of $10 to $15 per week. Once established, such programs came to be regarded as public responsibilities even after the economic crisis eased. Here, an NYA worker assists a doctor examining children at the St. Simon's Center at 22nd and Reed Streets in South Philadelphia in April 1941. The Center—housed in a black Episcopalian church—obviously made no attempt to challenge established patterns of racial segregation. Another NYA worker (below) supervises nursery school children at mealtime at the Germantown Settlement in March 1939. The three thousand Philadelphia NYA workers each received $20 per month along with job training. The other scenes are of the WPA Sewing Project, in which women who were generally too sick or too old to hold down regular full-time work produced clothing for hospitals and other charities. After several years of gradual reductions, the state notified the project's last twenty-seven hundred Philadelphia employees early in 1941 of its intent to close the operation. On the eve of the scheduled shutdown, the state gave project workers—including the group pictured opposite, who worked at 26th and Reed—a two-month reprieve. The expression on the face of Mrs. Pauline Spivak before learning that her job was still safe is a vivid illustration of what many of New Deal programs came to mean to the people who worked on them.

New Deal cultural programs also flourished in Philadelphia by the late 1930s. Particularly popular was the Federal Music Project. Though the WPA Symphony—with its Sunday afternoon concerts at Temple's Mitten Hall and the University of Pennsylvania's Irvine Auditorium—was its best-known local component, other parts of the project also gave work to musicians. The City Council Ensemble (above, left) plays for an appreciative audience at the Jewish Cultural Center on Marshall Street in January 1938. Through the WPA Symphony, the NYA's jazz bands and Negro Chorus, the Composers' Forum-Laboratory, and concerts like this, the Music Project became an integral part of the city's cultural life. The local Writers and Theater Projects each

employed more than a hundred people by 1937, while Art Project workers installed new galleries and period rooms at the Art Museum. Writers Project typists work on the Philadelphia volume in the American Guide Series (above, right). Two years in the making, the Guide required the efforts of 240 people for its publication in December 1937. This photograph reveals how WPA cultural programs had practical aims in training clerical as well as blue-collar workers. Some WPA programs were more directly targeted at the poorest parts of the population. In an Academic and Home Arts class WPA teachers taught black women basic literacy and home economics in their homes. The photograph at the top of the facing page was taken at 12th and Carpenter in one of the city's poorest neighborhoods. To the right, David Sundelson, at a Literacy and

Citizenship class at 3012 Cumberland Street in Strawberry Mansion, was one of more than five thousand immigrants tutored by the WPA between 1936 and 1940. By then, the WPA's educational and recreational programs employed six hundred teachers and had reached seventy-five thousand students. While most New Deal programs were controversial, the cultural programs drew particular criticism, including an investigation by the House Un-American Activities Committee. Conservatives faulted the programs because many were openly critical of the status quo —especially capitalism and racial segregation—and because they were targeted at those neglected by established cultural institutions.

The growing strength of organized labor paralleled, and often sustained, the city's New Deal programs. Philadelphia had long been a stronghold of the traditional craft unions of the American Federation of Labor. But in the 1920s the city had acquired a national reputation as a graveyard of industrial unionism. That changed dramatically with the enactment in June 1933 of the National Industrial Recovery Act, which protected workers' rights to organize and bargain collectively. Over the next year thousands of Philadelphia-area industrial workers organized unions and went on strike. But labor victories did not come easily. Below, Hosiery Workers Union pickets and police battle outside the M & M Knitting Mills at A and Indiana in Kensington. In their

efforts to protect workers defying the strike, the police encountered union supporters from forty-five local mills. The ensuing melee spread for six blocks around the plant and ended with dozens of injuries and forty-seven arrests. As even the anti-union Philadelphia *Evening Bulletin* noted, local residents closed their doors to strike-breakers trying to flee the union men. Though the results of the textile strikes of 1934 were mixed, organizing continued, and by mid-1935 some two hundred and fifty Philadelphia locals claimed a quarter of a million members. Many large industries and recalcitrant factories remained unorganized, however, until the Committee for (later Congress of) Industrial Organization (CIO) began its militant campaigns in 1936. Staging its first

local sit-down strike in January 1937, the CIO had ten thousand members by spring and sit-down strikes were spreading throughout the city.

An April sit-down strike at the Artcraft Silk Hosiery Mill at M Street and Torresdale Avenue—part of the CIO campaign—is dramatically documented on the next page (top). On the night of April 20, 1937, pickets overpowered 25 policemen and forced their way into the deserted plant. Within a few days their number swelled to 350. The company conceded a month later and gave its 780 employees union wages and working conditions. The success of these tactics encouraged imitation, and two weeks after the Artcraft seizure, more than two thousand workers went on strike at Apex Hosiery

at 5th and Luzerne, the largest non-union hosiery plant left in the city. Backed by five thousand demonstrators, about two hundred and fifty workers fought through a police cordon and took over the plant, where they remained for three months. Below, strikers and supporters are shown outside the mill on June 22. Supporters brought in food and other necessities—and even movies—from union headquarters. Overwhelming local support for the strikers in working-class Kensington made efforts to oust the strikers by force unwise. Apex finally capitulated on July 30. The struggle had been bitter, but through such victories workers like those pictured here finally made organized labor a powerful force in Philadelphia.

Over the course of the Depression, American political life became intensely politicized; activism spilled out of the labor movement and traditional political issues into wholly unrelated areas. Neighborhood residents, for example, had learned that the best way to get results was to take to the streets in highly visible demonstrations. Above, children block the intersection of 36th and Mount Vernon Streets in West Philadelphia in July 1938 in an effort to get a sprinkler. The signs and tactics of this integrated group successfully drew

media attention. At right, top, Federal Writers Project employees used a similarly dramatic approach when faced with February 1939 termination notices. Fifty workers from the Writers, Music, Theater, and Education Projects marched around City Hall carrying four coffins in a mock funeral organized by the radical Workers Alliance. As was common in such crises, they received a last-minute reprieve.

Funding problems also led the Building Trades Council to call a mass meeting on Reyburn Plaza (at right) to protest City Council's narrow defeat of the Philadelphia Housing Authority's $19 million construction budget in June 1940. The joint demonstration of thousands of construction workers and ideological proponents of public housing illustrated the powerful alliance between organized labor and public spending that resulted from the New Deal. The Tenants League banner behind the more sedate signs of the AFL Elevator Operators Union suggests that radicalism had become routine in 1930s Philadelphia.

The threat of war began to overshadow economic problems as political turmoil in Europe rippled through Philadelphia's ethnic communities in the late 1930s. Especially controversial were the activities of the German-American Bund, founded in 1933 after the Nazis seized power in Germany; the Bund's pro-Nazi politics found a small but vocal following in the area. By the mid-1930s, the Bund was publishing a newspaper, holding drills and rallies in the area around 6th and Erie, and maintaining a semimilitary camp near Perkasie in Bucks County. Bund members rallying at Reyburn Plaza in October 1936 (below) tried to link Nazi politics and American patriotism. Political passions rose over the next year and a half as many Philadelphians found themselves caught up in the Spanish Civil War, the growing persecution of German Jews, Mussolini's expansionist adventures in Africa, and Hitler's threats against his European neighbors. In February 1938, the Liederstafel Sangebund Hall, used as a drill room and beer garden by the Bund, was bombed. The photographs on the opposite page were taken a month later at a Bund meeting at Turngemeinde Hall at Broad and Columbia.

About a hundred pickets from the Citizen's Anti-Nazi Committee suddenly broke ranks and ran up to the third-floor meeting room. A fight ensued (below), and the police finally broke up the meeting. Despite growing public hostility and raids by the FBI, the Bund continued to be active until the United States entered the war. The FBI reported in 1940 that eight thousand people in the Philadelphia area had been active in the organization.

Many Philadelphians identified personally with victims of German and Japanese aggression. Some protested in the streets, others lobbied politicians, took in refugees, or became more assertive about their ethnic identity. Members of the normally reticent Chinese community march down Race Street near 10th in October 1937 (top of facing page). The parade—commemorating the twenty-sixth anniversary of the Chinese Republic—also called attention to Japan's attack on China. As marchers made their way around Chinatown, residents threw thousands of dollars for Chinese war victims into the mouth of its "dragon." The community then gathered to denounce Japanese aerial attacks on Chinese civilians. A year later, the focus was on Czechoslovakia's Sudentenland. At the left, Andrew Pajker of 6th and Fairmount reads about Neville Chamberlain's first visit to Hitler in September 1938. Though Philadelphia's Czechs were relatively prosperous, they were too few to do much more than read about the fate of their homeland. Members of the city's much larger Jewish community had relatives trying to flee Germany, Austria, and the growing list of lands under Nazi occupation. A few fortunate refugees soon began to appear in Philadelphia. In the photograph above, the family of J. Gerson Brenner of 4th and Dickinson welcomes refugees to their April 1939 Passover Seder. Seated on the far right are Fanny and Arnold Becker, who had left Vienna after the Nazi takeover the previous year. Links with immigrant homelands, vividly personified by the Beckers, brought the troubles of the late 1930s home to many Philadelphians.

By decade's end, marches of the unemployed had given way to very different demonstrations. In this photograph, papier-mâché effigies of Hitler, Mussolini, a caricatured Japanese, Britain's Neville Chamberlain, and France's Edouard Daladier tower above a large crowd at the 1939 May Day rally in Reyburn Plaza. The rally's popular front slogan—"Unite Against Fascism"—as well as the signs supporting the campaign of the Communist-dominated National Maritime Union against the oil companies emphasize that this was essentially a display of the impressive strength of the Philadelphia Communist Party in 1939. Organizers claimed that 15 unions and 185 other groups participated in this rally, which ended in the singing of the "Internationale." But the Party's strength had peaked when this photograph was taken, and the Clothing Workers' Union —the city's largest—was already boycotting the May Day parade because of Communist domination. Stalin's pact with Hitler only four months later reversed the American Communist Party's foreign policy and crippled the Party. At the 1941 May Day rally at Ontario Park at 13th and Thompson, shown on page 110, pennants sup-porting Communist Party leader Earl Browder shared center-stage with signs demanding that America stay out of the war. This rally attracted fewer than a thousand people and no major union support. Seven weeks later Germany attacked the Soviet Union and the signs at Communist demonstrations changed again to reflect the Party's new campaign for American intervention. Most Philadelphians reacted to the approach of war with anxiety and confusion rather than with firm political convictions. A *Bulletin* photographer captured the scene from inside the paper's Filbert Street office (on page 111). The date was September 1, 1939. Germany had just invaded Poland, and the *Bulletin* was posting war news and tracking military movements on a map visible to passers-by. The faces of these Philadelphians staring into a troubled future eloquently reveal their fear, their foreboding, and their determination.

Homefront

World War II came to Philadelphia nearly two years before Pearl Harbor. As conflict spread in Europe, the Delaware Valley turned again into the arsenal of democracy, enjoying a prosperity that its people had not seen since World War I. The very industries and communities that had suffered most in the 1920s and the Great Depression rebounded, and the city of immigrants and industry once again assumed its historic role as one of the world's greatest manufacturing centers. Once America's soldiers began to fight, Philadelphians quickly grew accustomed to bond rallies, air raid alerts, scrap drives, rationing, price controls, swing shifts, and USOs. The war also brought an extraordinary unity to this nation of nations, and this city of immigrants. But the war was only to be an interlude, and both its economic benefits and its sense of common purpose were to disappear long before wartime losses stopped exacting their toll in human pain.

Even as the Germans were demonstrating the superiority of mobile armor in their spring 1940 sweep across France, the Baldwin Locomotive Works was tooling up to meet its first order for light tanks. Other local firms followed suit, converting rapidly to military production and bringing over a billion dollars in contracts into the region by the end of 1940. The Depression faded into memory as military mobilization revived the almost-dormant industrial base and area employment soared. By the time the United States formally declared war, more than five hundred area companies held substantial defense contracts.

Nicetown's Midvale Steel began turning out naval gun turrets and armor plate around the clock. On nearby Wissahickon Avenue, Bendix Aviation manufactured airplane instruments. Brill switched from streetcars to gun carriages, Budd from railroad cars to aircraft parts and ammunition, Disston from saws and tools to light armor plate, and Ardmore's Autocar from civilian trucks to military personnel carriers and antitank vehicles. Cramp's Shipyard reopened, joining the Philadelphia Navy Yard, Chester's Sun Ship, and Camden's New York Ship in rebuilding the navy and the merchant marine. The war spurred innovation, leading to the widespread adoption of such new technologies as Plexiglas from Rohm and Haas for airplane cockpits and turrets, and blood plasma from Sharp and Dohme. More conventional local industries—lumber, chemicals, tobacco, textiles, rubber, and food processing—also took on war work. Ultimately, more than thirty-five hundred plants in the region were turning out products for the war effort. When the "battle for production" peaked in 1944, one of four local workers was directly employed in making war materiel.

Working on a locomotive for Russia at
Baldwin's, 1943

Expanding production needs outstripped a labor force already depleted by the loss of younger men to the military services. Women and blacks—both historically restricted in their employment opportunities—took up some of the slack. Women were not new to industrial production in Philadelphia, but they had generally been limited to textiles, the needle trades, food processing, and such light assembly work as the manufacture of small electrical appliances. During the war, such employment grew, but women moved into traditionally male jobs as well. "Rosie the Riveters" by the thousands took up heavy industrial work in the metal trades, shipbuilding, and chemicals. The number of women with manufacturing jobs locally doubled by 1944, at which point nearly four in ten workers were female. Discrimination against blacks—long even more pervasive than that against women—also eased and, grudgingly, Philadelphia's black workforce doubled by 1944. White male workers, however, fearful of losing work after the war, resented the growing presence of both blacks and women in manufacturing jobs.

The city's industrial capacity quickly outgrew the local labor pool. Well-paid jobs in war industry—particularly in shipbuilding—drew tens of thousands of workers into the Delaware Valley. This stream of workers carried thousands of southern blacks, whose earlier migration had slowed to a trickle in the Depression.

Migration, like wartime prosperity, revived the Depression-wracked housing industry. The Northeast and South Philadelphia began to grow again, and new housing appeared in the northern and western suburbs. But the building boom was short lived. Soon after the United States entered the war, federal priorities restricted housing construction to the war effort. Regulations on the private use of lumber followed, and by 1943 new houses were once again unavailable. Thousands of newcomers were forced into subdivided rowhouses, and others had to double up or move into trailer camps. Blacks particularly suffered. They occupied fewer than one hundred of the more than eleven thousand houses built during the short boom. Crowding into the oldest structures, they were most affected by the suspension of housing and sanitary code enforcement dictated by the need to accommodate defense workers.

Food and fuel were also in short supply in Philadelphia as elsewhere and subject to a complex and imperfectly administered rationing system. Local rationing boards took need, health considerations, and such special circumstances as an individual's relation to the war effort into account in issuing the books of coupons and the stickers required for the purchase of certain commodities. Starting with only a few items essential to war production, rationing eventually covered meats, fats, sugar, cigarettes, shoes, coffee, butter, rubber, liquor, and gasoline. Flourishing black markets in almost all these commodities entered the folklore of the homefront, and periodic investigations and raids enlivened the war years.

Rationing served many purposes. As incomes rose while consumer products remained relatively scarce, rationing helped contain inflation. It also suspended the free market of supply and demand, assuring even those who were not well off that they could get necessities. And rationing spread sacrifice throughout the community, giving citizens the impression, at least, that they were helping win the war.

Banners hung in rowhouse windows offered a far more poignant testimony to wartime sacrifice. A blue star meant a child in the service; a gold one meant a relative lost in battle. Nearly a quarter-million local men registered when the draft began in late 1940. More than one hundred and eighty thousand Philadelphia men and women saw active duty; and more than one hundred thousand came from the five suburban counties. The region lost five thousand dead and about half that number missing in action. With casualties more numerous at war's end than at its outset, morale ebbed even as victory neared in 1944 and 1945.

Homefront morale was a constant concern for the government. Realizing that the war's outcome would as surely be determined in the factories of cities like Philadelphia as on Pacific islands, North African deserts, or French beaches, government officials developed strategies to build support for the war effort. Perhaps the most successful were bond drives, which let civilians share in financing the war even while draining the economy of billions of potentially inflationary dollars. Collections for the Red Cross, Victory Gardens, scrap drives, and armed forces displays had different objectives, but served the same general purpose. So too—once it became clear in 1942 that the continental United States was not likely to be invaded or bombed—did civil defense programs, blackouts, and air raid alerts. Airplane spotters all over the Delaware Valley scanned the skies for German planes long after the real danger had passed. But memories of tankers sunk within sight of the Jersey shore in 1942, and government propaganda about the vital service they were performing, kept them alert.

Yet there were problems on the homefront. Philadelphia was full of divided families and lonely wives; social service agencies wrestled with marital difficulties and the plight of children left without supervision because their mothers were war workers. At the same time, thousands of servicemen and women poured into the city on weekends from Fort Dix and McGuire Air Force Base in nearby New Jersey to join naval personnel on shore leave. All were bent on having a good time, perhaps their last good time, and that put great pressure on law enforcement agencies and created problems for the civilian population. Strangers drawn to the city for work or military assignments brought other morale problems, as did lengthened work weeks and shortages of consumer goods. Workers grew increasingly restless as the war dragged on, and labor militancy—which had gone into abeyance with the first flush of wartime patriotism—resurfaced in 1944 with walkouts by teamsters and longshoremen and strikes at Sun Ship, Cramp's, and SKF Industries, firms vital to the defense effort. Tensions in the workplace heightened in 1944 when the War Manpower Commission declared a labor shortage in Philadelphia, ordered war workers onto a minimum work week of forty-eight hours, and prohibited half a million workers from leaving their jobs. At one point, the Quartermaster Corps had to rely on German war prisoners to do its work.

The labor shortage exploded when the Philadelphia Transit Company—needing workers and responding to a hesitant federal commitment to civil rights—hired blacks in the traditionally white-only jobs of motorman and conductor. White transit workers struck and rioted, disrupting war production as no previous homefront event had. President Roosevelt was forced to divert ten thousand fully armed troops from the invasion of Europe to patrol the city and get the trolleys running.

Fortunately for Philadelphians, the wartime economy brought relatively easy money, providing some relief from wartime anxiety and sacrifice. But there were no washing machines, refrigerators, or radios in the stores, and the last car rolled off the assembly line in February 1942. With consumer goods limited, workers could pay off Depression-era debts, save, or spend on recreation and entertainment. Attendance at the movies went up dramatically. Many chose escape. Philadelphians thronged to the Jersey shore and the Poconos—mostly by train and bus because of gas rationing—and to local parks and playgrounds. Cultural life and sports teams stayed close to their peacetime schedules, though by 1944 with most of the stars in the service, major-league baseball was of minor-league caliber. Nightclubs did well, and the war years saw the highest attendance ever recorded at area racetracks.

Philadelphia contributed more than its share to the war effort. But the war returned only an artificial prosperity to the region and did little to stem the underlying economic decline that had predated the Great Depression. Wartime prosperity did not check the city's eroding industrial base, its physical deterioration, or the growing impoverishment of much of its population. The genuine joy that greeted American victory soon gave way to the realization that Philadelphia faced an uncertain future.

The coming of war made itself felt in Philadelphia's many communities. As the production of military supplies for Britain and for the nation's defense revived long-dormant industries, Philadelphia employment rose from 763,000 in January 1940 to an all-time high of 959,000 in October 1941. German submarine activity in the North Atlantic provided a special stimulus to shipbuilding. Kensington's reopened Cramp's Shipyard, pictured at left, launched its first ship on August 2, 1941. More impressive warships followed this modest YR29 floating repair barge as Cramp's eventually turned out five cruisers, fourteen submarines, and more than twenty other ships for the navy. But as some men returned to work, others entered military service. Philadelphia's first draftees—inducted in an elaborate ceremony at the Liberty Bell on November 25, 1940—are shown above right, on their way to basic training at Fort Meade, Maryland. Somber reminders of war's dislocations also appeared in the city. Many Philadelphians sent aid packages to Britons enduring the Blitz. And portrayed here, to the right, are some Jewish refugees from Nazi atrocities who—through a rare combination of luck and persistence—managed to reach the city by freighter from Portugal in late 1941. The attack on Pearl Harbor thus found Philadelphians already acquainted with the excitement and the horror of World War II.

Philadelphia's skilled workforce and strong industrial base of foundries and workshops, mills and factories made the city a center of military production. Underutilized plants and underemployed workers turned to producing tanks, airplanes, ordnance, and materiel. Factories like the Baldwin Locomotive Works, which had been too large to produce efficiently for a shrinking civilian market, were perfectly suited for the massive demands of the military, as the July 1941 scene above of two parallel assembly lines for medium tanks attests. Opposite, a photograph documenting the pouring of tons of molten steel for 75mm

tank gun tubes at Manayunk's Empire Ordnance in November 1941 celebrates heavy industries, which the war made crucial to the nation once again. By war's end, the Philadelphia ordnance district, which extended into North Carolina but centered on the Delaware Valley, had produced more than 19,200 tanks and 44,800 artillery pieces and anti-aircraft guns, as well as 25 million shells. The local tradition of craftsmanship in small enterprises also played an important role in the defense effort. At right, Nathan Benson, a

Russian immigrant who worked at the Philadelphia Mint, applies a micrometer to a bronze bevel gear casting in his West Philadelphia home workshop in May 1943. This was one of the hundreds of such operations in the area. From the Baldwin Works to Nathan Benson's basement, the war years represented the last great achievement of Philadelphia's industrial power and skilled workmanship.

121

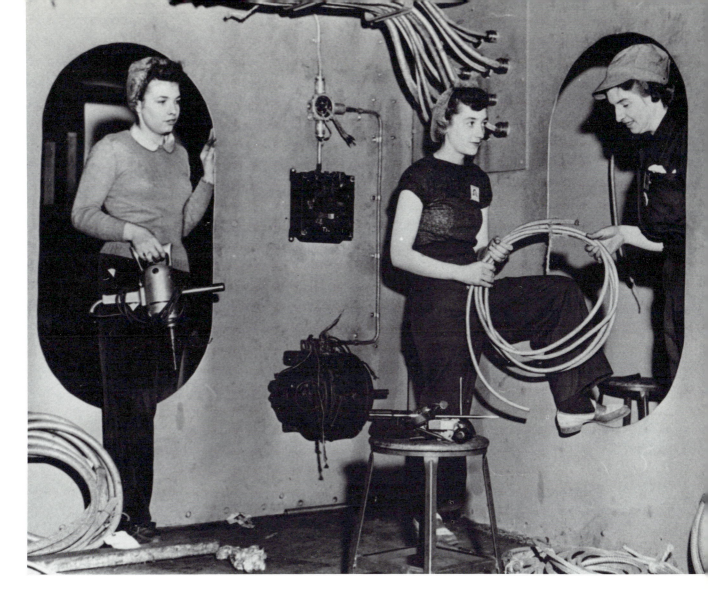

Job opportunities for women widened as thousands of men entered the military services. Initially, these were service positions; only afterwards did women move into industrial jobs previously closed to them. At left, Pearl Gold delivers milk for the Supplee Milk Company in Bryn Mawr, and Frances Heisler is a service station attendant for Atlantic Refining in Philadelphia, both in June 1943. Human-interest pictures of women doing "men's jobs" were a staple of wartime photojournalism. These two photographs were taken by Jack Delano, who formerly worked for the Farm Security Administration. Then with the Office of War Information, he was instructed to take upbeat pictures of ordinary Americans aiding the war effort. Eventually, labor shortages opened positions in heavy industry, skilled trades, and military construction to women, though "Rosie the Riveter" types were always a small minority of the female labor force during the war. Above, Regina Freek and Mrs. Henry Cornue of Northeast Philadelphia and Agnes O'Neal of Norristown train to be electricians' helpers at the Navy Yard in February 1943. By May 1944, the three hundred thousand women working outside their homes in the Philadelphia area made up 27 percent of all munitions workers and 48 percent of the industrial workforce outside the munitions factories.

The government's public relations apparatus placed countless stories in newspapers documenting the contribution of women to the war effort. Typically, these linked a woman's war work, her continued domestic responsibilities and pleasures, and her relationship to a man in military service. Taken by the federal government's Office for Emergency Management in March 1942, these photographs document the life of Eva Smuda, a Polish immigrant who was a widowed mother of six and worked at the Frankford Arsenal making anti-aircraft shells. These photographs show her living with her daughter, granddaughter, and son-in-law, who also worked at the nearby Arsenal. Her son in the Army had sent her the memento from Fort Bragg shown at the right. The government's captions explained that she enjoyed giving half a day to her home and half a day to her country. These carefully posed images provide an idealized picture of an American mother contributing to the war effort while maintaining her traditional role at home.

The same labor shortages that opened traditional men's jobs to women gave blacks access to jobs previously restricted to whites. After President Roosevelt, under considerable pressure, signed the Fair Employment Practices order in June 1941, military contractors and military bases offered some of the best opportunities for blacks. Benjamin Stephens is shown at the far left using a pneumatic chipper on a ship propeller at the Navy Yard in 1942. Next to him, the 1943 image of Beatrice Paul illustrates the growing range of jobs available to blacks. The Office of War Information photographed her working on a generator at the Yellow Cab garage as part of a series extolling the advances made by blacks during the war. But the 1944 photograph above of a supply loading unit camped at Broad and Pattison in South Philadelphia reveals another face of the wartime racial situation, the continuing segregation of the American armed forces.

Tensions created by the entry of blacks into jobs previously restricted to whites came to a head in the 1944 Philadelphia Transit Company strike. Blacks had demanded that discriminatory transit union contract provisions be set aside so that they could become motormen—spelling out their arguments in the November 1943 demonstration shown here. When protracted negotiations finally led to the start of training for blacks as motormen and conductors on buses and trolleys in August 1944, white workers struck in protest, paralyzing the transit system. Defense industries resorted to such emergency measures as the shuttle truck (pictured on page 130) carrying workers to the Frankford Arsenal to keep it operating. On August 5, President Roosevelt sent several thousand troops to make sure the transit system ran and threatened to draft striking workers. On page 131, soldiers are on guard at the 10th and Luzerne car barn (above), and the first car to resume service on August 7, is a Route 53 streamliner, complete with military escort (below). Within ten days the strike was broken, and the blacks kept their new jobs. But the events of August 1944 hardly bode well for postwar race relations.

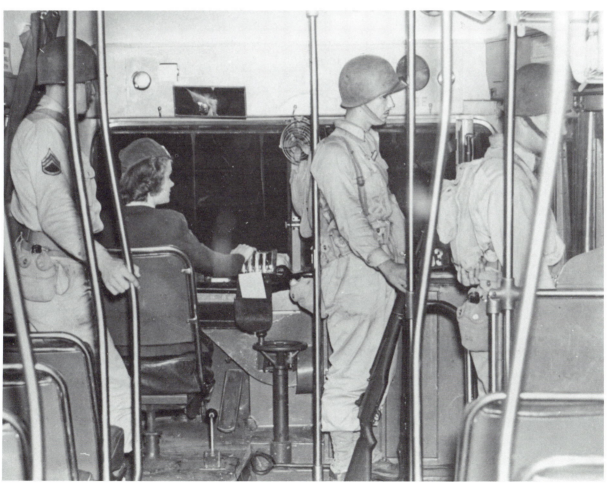

America's haphazard wartime rationing system intruded into the daily lives of many Philadelphians. Shortages, military needs, and profiteering forced the government to extend rationing in January 1942 from sugar to coffee, canned goods, and gasoline; by spring 1943, meats, fish, fats, oils, and cheese had been added to the list. People grumbled endlessly about the complex and ever-changing system of ration books, stamps, and points for different commodities, but the photograph above of housewives protesting high prices in August 1942 at 30th and York reveals the conditions that led to rationing. A year later, butter—because of military demands and the diversion of cream supplies to more profitable uses—had become the scarcest of all rationed goods. One typical result, shown on the top of the next page, was the 8 PM line at Frankford and Cottman in response to word that Saler's Dairy had received a rare shipment of butter. Gas rationing was handled better, though attempts to cheat were common. Workers were assigned A, B, or C ration books according to their war contribution and/or the number of people they drove to work. Nonessential A-level workers could initially buy enough gas to travel about 240 miles per month; B- and C-level classifications were highly prized. To the right, officials of the Office of Price Administration, the unpopular rationing agency, check the stickers and ration books of drivers on Broad Street below Callowhill in May 1943. Despite rationing and regulations, most Americans suffered comparatively little privation during the war.

Decent housing was in short supply in wartime Philadelphia. With employment rising and automobile commuting limited because of rationing, thousands of war workers scrambled for accommodations near defense plants located in long-congested neighborhoods. Overcrowding, evictions, and rent gouging were commonplace. The government imposed rent control in mid-1942 as an emergency measure and built defense housing projects throughout the Delaware Valley. The nearly twelve thousand local units included such temporary projects as the Tacony, League Island, and Shipyard Homes. Permanent projects included Pennypack Woods, Abbotsford Homes, and Bartram Village in Philadelphia; Lamokin and McCaffrey Villages in Chester; and Ablett and Audubon Villages in Camden County, New Jersey. Above, sailors help Mrs. Bernard Kitzinger, wife of a Navy Yard worker, move into Passyunk Homes at 24th and Packer in South Philadelphia only a week before Pearl Harbor. The 1,000-unit project was designed for defense workers making between $1,200 and $2,600 per year. But with government efforts proving inadequate, private house construction suspended, and the city gaining population, large trailer camps became increasingly common in industrial areas. At the right, a mother keeps house and tends children in a camp of five hundred trailers on MacDade Boulevard in Chester in August 1942.

Fears of aerial bombing and sabotage led many Philadelphians to participate in wartime civil defense. The first two scenes date from December 1941, when alarm swept through the nation in the wake of Pearl Harbor. At left, children at Northwest School, Race and Carlisle Streets, sit through an air raid drill in their school corridors. Below, a police officer explains the proper way to handle an unexploded bomb to a group of teachers at the Fleisher Vocational School at 13th and Wood. Though fears soon eased, elaborate air raid precautions continued. Sirens by the hundreds were put up along the city's streets; by late 1943 fifty thousand citizens had enlisted as air raid wardens or emergency workers. Air raid drills cleared the streets and periodically bathed the city in darkness until October 1943. Opposite, a typical blackout scene in February 1942 shows center city at dusk from the Free Library at 19th and the Parkway. Even after blackouts ended in 1943, motorists had to drive at night with low beams and the top half of their headlights painted over. An elaborate civil defense program remained in place until the end of the war, by then more for morale than defense.

Military displays and rallies—among them bond drives that built civilian morale and raised over $3 billion in Philadelphia—were a regular feature of the war years. Above, a benefit appearance by Bob Hope and Bing Crosby at Strawbridge & Clothier in May 1943 was one of the many that major radio and film stars made in this city. Opposite, a September 1943 bond rally of RCA employees is held in Camden. RCA was booming and the pay packets of its workers were a tempting target for government fundraisers. Other boosts to morale came when American units marched in formation through the city's streets. Rarely were they so well juxtaposed with Hollywood's war effort as in this August 1943 scene in front of the Mastbaum Theater at 20th and Market (page 140). Perhaps the greatest morale builder was America's wartime leader, Franklin Roosevelt, shown arriving at Shibe Park for an election rally on October 27, 1944. Even in Philadelphia, still controlled locally by a Republican machine, Franklin Roosevelt's wartime appearances were great festive occasions.

The government sought ways to make people feel involved in the war effort. Families were encouraged to grow vegetables in Victory Gardens; nearly a hundred thousand Philadelphians did so, easing the potential shortage of fresh food. A model Victory Garden was constructed in 1943 at 21st and the Parkway (at the right). Even children were galvanized in domestic campaigns; scrap drives were a special case in point. A shortage of scrap metal in the fall of 1942 threatened steel production, and in a frantic three-week campaign people were encouraged to bring junk metal of all kinds as well as rubber to collection points. A group of children brings a typical load to Franklin Field in return for free admission to a University of Pennsylvania football game (below). At the end of the three weeks, the shortage was declared over; Pennsylvania's contribution was 111 pounds of metal for every person in the Commonwealth. Though enthusiasm flagged later in the war, such activities as Victory Gardens and scrap drives gave people the feeling that they could contribute to the war effort, and left many citizens with memories of what they did as children to help win World War II.

The war altered normal routines on the homefront and exposed many to new experiences. Thousands of Philadelphians worked midnight-to-8 AM "graveyard shifts" at plants producing war materiel around the clock. They inevitably formed their own subculture. Left, Budd Company munitions workers dance at a July 1943 "graveyard shift jamboree" at 3rd and Mentor Streets in Olney, in one of several "nightclubs" where employees could unwind after work in the hours before noon. The area's several dozen USO centers also hosted parties, as well as offering a range of services from counseling to overnight rooms for soldiers and sailors stationed in an unfamiliar city. Below, two sailors and two local girls bob for apples at the 1944 Halloween party at the Camden USO, a scene typical of the image of wholesome enjoyment which the USO generally conveyed.

Not all wartime social life was wholesome. Soldiers and sailors from such nearby bases as Fort Dix and the Navy Yard sometimes brought downtown Philadelphia the kinds of problems normally found in smaller military towns. Military Police and the Shore Patrol regularly swept through the prospering vice district northeast of City Hall, often breaking up fights, while authorities struggled with the threats posed by alcoholism and venereal disease. Throngs of servicemen drifted around the city, their attentions not always unwelcome to young women whose boyfriends were gone for the duration. The Philadelphia *Bulletin* was concerned enough about the transformation of City Hall courtyard into a hangout that it ran these photographs of the area in May 1942. These were among the few unflattering views of servicemen published during the war. The newspaper presented even these photographs circumspectly, noting that the crowd of sailors was in the courtyard at 6 PM for the "dating hour."

While the war commanded the nation's energies, it did not fundamentally disrupt many of the essential continuities of urban life. The mixture of old and new, which was the legacy of the booming twenties and the depressed thirties, remained frozen in place in Philadelphia's rowhouse neighborhoods for the duration. Above is a classical old-fashioned scene at 5th and Bainbridge, where carriage drivers brought their horses to a watering trough. John Ebstel, a photographer documenting South Philadelphia slums in 1941 and 1942 for the Housing Association, captured more typical neighborhood scenes, eloquently reminding us, in his views of stoop-sitting, of the rowhouses on the 200 block of McKean Street, and of mothers and children in Dickinson Square, that amid war work, air raid drills, bond drives, and rationing, life often went on as it had before Pearl Harbor for many Philadelphians.

It was not always easy to maintain normal life during the war. Though President Roosevelt had declared that major-league baseball should continue with its regular schedule, many regular ballplayers had entered the service and wartime baseball featured an odd assortment of overage or militarily unfit players. Because Philadelphia was still a two-team city, baseball was played at Shibe Park almost every day from April through September during the entire war. The photograph at the left from an August 1943 Athletics–White Sox game shows the end of a botched double play by the home team, a not untypical scene in wartime baseball. The June 1944 graduating class of Girls High, pictured below, was more successful in preserving normality. In the spirit of the common reprimand "Don't you know there's a war on?" school administrators had decreed that corsages made of war stamps would be more appropriate than the traditional flowered procession. Students protested and won their point. Such small battles reflect the need people felt occasionally to be free of the war.

Americans on the homefront were able to enjoy themselves in ways unimaginable to their allies and enemies. With their earnings increasing, Philadelphians crowded the Jersey shore and the Poconos in the summer and movies and nightclubs all year long. Below, the July 4th, 1943, crush at the Market Street ferry was intense. The war boosted travel to the nearby shore because gas rationing prevented longer trips, but that also meant that the ferries and the trains to the shore were more crowded than in peacetime. To the right, a predominantly young Saturday matinee audience waits for the double feature at the Savoia Theater at Broad and Morris in South Philadelphia in April 1942. More parents had enough money to let their children go to the movies than during the Depression, but with more mothers working outside the home there was criticism that the movies were becoming substitute parents, with "latchkey" children wasting days in the theaters. The photograph on the facing page shows one leisure-time consequence of the migration of over thirty thousand blacks to Philadelphia during the war. The *Bulletin* captioned this July 1945 scene at South Philadelphia's League Island Pool "99 and 44/100 percent colored." The war had integrated many jobs, but it had not disturbed social segregation.

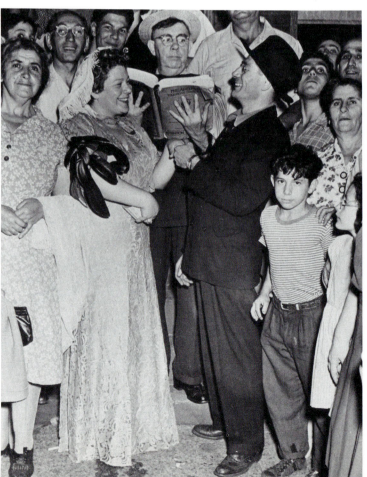

Philadelphia's celebration of the victory over Nazi Germany in May 1945 was relatively subdued, since people expected the war in the Pacific would continue for two more years. But thousands did mark the event in downtown streets, including the crowd that gathered along Market Street east of City Hall, as shown in the photograph to the left. The celebration of the sudden surrender of Japan after the atomic bombing in August was much more exuberant. The whole city stopped for several days and spontaneous parties broke out in many neighborhoods. To the left, below, a mock wedding, a folk custom marking personal or social transitions—in this case the end of the war—takes place on V-J Day in the 2100 block of North Corliss Street in Strawberry Mansion. Martin Kilcourse poses as a minister, phonebook "Bible" in hand, to "marry" Sylvia Rabinowitz and Samuel Kaplan, two of his neighbors. With victory, many wartime restrictions quickly ended. By August 19, the end of gas rationing brought enough cars out to Fairmount Park to merit running the photograph below in the *Inquirer*.

Family Album, World War II

A Fourth of July parade in 1942 on Roosevelt Boulevard near Rising Sun Avenue. These are volunteer firemen organized as a civil defense unit, ready to respond in case of an enemy attack on Philadelphia.

Joe Keys and Johnny Hahn on leave in 1943 in front of the Keys's home in the 3000 block of Water Street in Kensington. Keys was too heavy to enlist in the Army, Navy, or Marines but finally was able to join the Merchant Marine. Hahn was in the 101st Airborne Division. This was his last visit home; he was killed in Belgium shortly after the Normandy invasion in 1944.

In the picture to the left is David Kendis, home on leave in 1942. His mother is on the right and a friend on the left. They are standing in front of Kendis Slip Covers at 2034 Germantown Avenue. Above, Evelyn Carrowon Robinson is sitting on a bread delivery box at the corner of Belgrade and Berks Streets in Kensington with Dolen Hill, a sailor from Alabama stationed in Philadelphia.

A well-dressed young lady during wartime. Elsie Kendis, née Silberman, at C Street and Wyoming Avenue in the winter of 1944, showing off a silver-tipped racoon coat.

This snapshot of a young couple with their young son was taken on the porch of 1323 North 7th Street in the summer of 1943 just before the husband was drafted into the army. Note the cars and the unique porches.

Just hanging out has always been a favorite Philadelphia pastime and a frequent subject for photographs. Here, two teenage girls in front of the candy store at the corner of 3rd and Shunk Streets in the summer of 1941. Note the bobby sox and skirt lengths.

Another Philadelphia cowboy. This one is Tom Curry riding on Upland Street in Southwest Philadelphia on his birthday in the summer of 1942.

A 1944 photograph of Mr. and Mrs. Leonard Wagner in their backyard Victory Garden at 4476 Salmon Street, in the Bridesburg section of the city.

A Frankford YWCA co-ed party at Clementine Lake in New Jersey in the summer of 1941. Betty Bachman Jenkins, who owns the photo, is second from the left in the bottom row. The war separated the group and made this kind of gathering a rare occurrence. The photo below of four young bathing beauties without men was taken at the Boulevard Pool on Roosevelt Boulevard below Cottman Avenue in June 1944. Left to right are Eleanor Koenig Keyser, Marjorie Beers Poole, Betty Kovach White, and Susanna Key Norbury.

Young children remained a favorite subject for photographs during the war. But even children were touched by the patriotism of wartime. The young sailor is thirteen-month-old Stephen McWilliams sitting on the steps at 4614 North Palethorp Street in 1944. The girl in the flag-decorated stroller is Rosalie Ellen Brooks on her first birthday in September 1942. Her sister Naomi stands beside her.

Seven-year-old Elizabeth Grabowski playing the piano in her home on Waverly Road in Laverock, Cheltenham Township in 1945. The piano was an important symbol of middle-class standing as well as a place to display family photos.

A Last Hurrah

The end of the war led Philadelphians to hope that they could resume their normal lives. The generation that had grown up in the shadow of the Depression and come of age defending the nation in a globe-spanning conflict was powerfully attracted to the storybook ideal of settling down and living happily ever after. The traditional values and simple pleasures of home and family promised security and happiness after a decade and a half of turmoil.

Marriages delayed by economic hardship or wartime uncertainty were the order of the day for returning troops. Likewise most women who had shouldered historically male jobs in war industries returned to more traditional feminine domestic pursuits. Some did not abandon the labor force voluntarily, but cultural norms, reinforced by a national policy fearful of a return to Depression-era unemployment and concerned with easing the reintegration of veterans into the economy, favored the resumption of longstanding sex roles and the reemphasis of family life. The number of marriage licenses issued in Philadelphia jumped by nearly 50 percent in a single year, reaching an all-time high of twenty-two thousand in 1946. After a long period of deprivation, making up for lost time became the keynote of the postwar era.

Divorces not surprisingly climbed to unprecedented levels at the same time. Many of the more than five thousand divorces recorded in the city in 1946 were likely the unfinished business of Depression and war. Some couples who could not afford to break up their homes in the 1930s because of the cost of maintaining separate households probably found that luxury within reach after the war. Other couples who followed wartime romances too hastily into matrimony discovered their incompatibility with postwar reunification. The surge in divorce also testified to the idealization of marriage. The insecurity of the Depression and the unpredictability of war had invested family life with almost magical qualities. But not all marriages could be special; those failing to meet the now-heightened expectations for happiness were at greater risk of dissolution.

The idealization of family life was most evident, however, in the marriages that worked, in the couples who found fulfillment in each other and in raising children. The nation's postwar baby boom reversed more than a century and a half of steady decline in childbearing. While the birth rate during the boom did not return to its nineteenth-century levels, children and home life moved to the center of the national imagination. Large families received favorable attention in magazines and movies. Ultimately, the baby boom would transform many aspects of American life.

Welcome home display in Kensington, 1946

But in the later 1940s, having children meant realizing traditional values and living out the dreams inherited from earlier generations.

The immediate postwar period was not yet the child-oriented culture of the 1950s, when the birth rate actually peaked. The children of the 1940s lived through their decade as small, not especially visible, and—except to their parents—not particularly demanding harbingers of things to come. Overcrowded schools and double shifts would constitute the educational crisis of the 1950s, but in the late 1940s Philadelphia school enrollments continued to shrink as they had done since mid-Depression.

It would also be several years before growing families pouring into new child-centered residential developments in Northeast Philadelphia and the suburbs put their stamp on the geography of the region. The city's most notable concentrations of new housing in the late 1940s were Oxford Circle in the northeast, the Temple Stadium area in the northwest corner, and Overbrook Park, bordering Cobbs Creek on the city's far western fringe. Across the city, new construction averaged only about six thousand housing units annually in the postwar 1940s; this was only half the yearly total of the mid-1920s. Korean War restrictions on new building imposed in 1951 cut short a recovery to pre-Depression levels that had begun in 1950.

The new postwar production of automobiles also took a few years before its full impact was felt. Cars had opened a suburban circle to settlement in the 1920s. In the decades after 1950 the suburban ring would once again explode outward, but in the late 1940s, the relationship of Philadelphians and their cars resembled the hesitant exploration accompanying the renewal of an old love affair. The first rediscovery of the automobile after Depression hardship and wartime gas rationing—tantalizingly suggested in 1946 with the first new car models in years—altered little how and where people lived. Rather, it led to a reliving of old pleasures fondly remembered. With rationing lifted, Philadelphians took to the road for recreation. The Easter and Fourth of July weekends in 1946 saw the heaviest shore traffic since 1941. But it took a longer period of readjustment to peacetime and prosperity before the automobile reached its full influence as a way of life, and its potential as a force to reshape the face of the city.

Suspended altogether during the war, national automobile production did not reach 1929 levels until 1949. Similarly, car registrations in Philadelphia rebounded after the war, but did not return to earlier levels until 1949—even then the majority of city families still did not own cars.

Highway construction had little visible impact on the city in the 1940s. The original Pennsylvania Turnpike, authorized in 1937 and completed in 1940 as a federal Public Works Administration project, reached from Harrisburg to Pittsburgh; begun in 1948, the Philadelphia end of the road only extended westward from King of Prussia, leaving the turnpike ring that most directly served the city—like the Schuylkill Expressway and the Roosevelt Boulevard Extension—for the 1950s. The city's two major Delaware River bridges—the Tacony-Palmyra, opened in 1929, and the Benjamin Franklin, opened in 1926—were exceptions to the general rule, recording a dramatic doubling of traffic between 1945 and 1949. The continuing collapse of ferry traffic accounted for little of this increase. It was rather that the bridges had been put in service just before the Depression struck; the late 1940s surge in use represented a decade and a half's delay in their effective openings.

It was even more clear in the industrial neighborhoods surrounding the city's core that the late 1940s were a reminder of times gone by. The once mighty textile and clothing industries continued the slide that had predated the Depression. Other local industries for which military contracts had meant a temporary reprieve from long-term decline—notably Baldwin Locomotive Works and Midvale Steel—laid off half or more of their employees; Cramp's Shipyard closed altogether. Cutbacks in government employment at the Frankford Arsenal, the Navy Yard, and the Quartermaster Corps cost tens of thousands of additional jobs.

The surge in unemployment at war's end was shortlived. Expansion of such industrial sectors as chemicals and petroleum—with the Delaware Valley consolidating its position as the nation's second-largest oil refining center—brought substantial recovery. But just as the recovery favored some segments of the diversified local economy over others, so too the postwar economic readjustment held different meanings for black and white workers. Long excluded from better jobs in the peacetime economy, blacks were especially hurt as wartime labor force shortages came to an end. When Sun Shipbuilding and Drydock contracted from thirty-four thousand jobs to fewer than four thousand, for example, blacks who had been recruited into skilled jobs as welders were laid off. Like many black former employees of other war-related industries, most could find no positions using their training and experience but had to settle for work as unskilled laborers or service workers.

The old order returned to the workplace in other ways as well. The war had cut short a rising tide of labor activism as a reinvigorated and sometimes radical union movement had rebuilt itself after a series of defeats in the 1920s. During the war itself, strong unions in such basic industries as electrical goods, steel, and machinery—capitalizing on a federally imposed system of cooperative labor–management relations designed to prevent work stoppages—had made further gains in local and national plants. With war's end, radicalized workers reasserted their Depression-era militance and restated their wartime expectations, demanding a voice in planning for peacetime conversion and seeking higher wages to offset the rising prices that followed the end of price controls. Veterans marched on City Hall and on Harrisburg in 1946, demanding a special session of the legislature to address issues of housing, unemployment, education, and health care. In the immediate postwar period, workers confronted manufacturers intent on rolling back labor's earlier gains, making the nationwide strike wave of 1945 and 1946 a reprise of Depression radicalism and struggle. Major industrial strikes in the Philadelphia area at General Electric, Westinghouse, Baldwin Locomotive, and Electric Storage Battery took place against the backdrop of more local walkouts by bakers, brewers, hotel workers, newspaper deliverymen, tugboat workers, and bus, subway, and trolley drivers and conductors.

The postwar surge of radical activity, coming as it did in an atmosphere of war-heightened patriotism, stimulated a conservative backlash. With hostility toward the Soviet Union growing, many Philadelphians joined with their fellow Americans in reasserting their loyalty. Thousands jammed the Freedom Train when it visited the city in the summer of 1947, carrying the Declaration of Independence, the Constitution, and other documents central to national identity. Philadelphians marched in annual Loyalty Day parades, carrying banners denouncing the Russians. A million and a half people watched the eleven-hour-long, August 1949 American Legion parade that newspapers called the greatest pageant in the city's history. By 1950, Mayor Bernard Samuel was calling for substantial local spending for civil defense and Pennsylvania's Governor James Duff was publicly advocating hanging American Communists. The unresolved conflicts of Depression and war ushered the city into the Cold War.

Similarly, the city's long history of political corruption and its century of accumulated physical decay set the stage for the stirrings of reform. The few New Deal projects had made only the barest dent in the local legacy of substandard and insufficient housing; the Depression downturn in business only emphasized the deterioration of the commercial core and the industrial districts. Likewise, Franklin Roosevelt's victories in the local vote count had not toppled the city's entrenched

Republican machine. Civic efforts to reform the structure of city government and address longstanding physical decay began to come to fruition in the years just after the war. The "Renaissance," as it came to be called, emerged gradually with a 1947 exhibit of what Philadelphia might be, gained speed in 1949 with the election victories of Joseph Clark as controller and Richardson Dilworth as treasurer, and became visible with the start of work on the Society Hill urban renewal project in the 1950s.

The beginnings of political reform and of planning efforts for the city's physical renewal represented important new departures. In the same optimistic spirit the city hoped to lure the permanent headquarters of the United Nations to Philadelphia and arranged for a subcommittee of the international organization to visit for several days in late 1946. With similar postwar exuberance, the Yellow Cab Company suggested helicopter routes between center city and the suburbs in the same year. More realistically and more successfully, thousands of individual Philadelphians welcomed the return of peace and prosperity by returning to school or by taking out mortgages for new houses under the GI Bill, and by starting record numbers of new businesses. Postwar readjustment was prelude as well as postscript.

Homecomings and joyous reunions greeted area servicemen at war's end. Army Engineers Italo Balducci of Scranton, John Skootla and Bernard Levin of Philadelphia, Thomas Sinclair of Clymer, and William Owens of Lansdowne on their way to reprocessing at Fort Kilmer, New Jersey, are shown above on the *Griswold*, docking at the Fort Mifflin supply depot September 22, 1945. Opposite, a month later, the battleship *Washington* led twenty-five warships—with eleven thousand crew members awaiting discharge— up the Delaware River for a triumphant Navy Day celebration. Demobilization dragged on well into 1946, sparking protests from soldiers and sailors eager to return to civilian life. Grassroots groups could often be more sensitive to servicemen than the military bureaucracy. On page 166, neighbors on Kensington's 2800 block of Jasper Street, who had formed a Serviceman's Community Chest to send presents overseas during the war, wound up their efforts in 1946 with a welcoming banquet and a $125 check for each returning veteran from the immediate neighborhood.

Memories of Depression unemployment linked with the desire of veterans to make up for lost time lent a special urgency to postwar education; in the first year after the war alone, this area recorded more than one hundred thousand applications for training or education programs under the GI Bill. Eager veterans flooded local schools and colleges. Below, veterans, including a former WAVE, attend a November 1945 algebra class at Temple University High School.

Haverford College increased its enrollment from four to five hundred to accommodate veterans, many of whom studied engineering and science. On the following page, veterans attending Haverford in October 1946 pick up practical skills in the machine shop. Most of the more than one hundred bricklaying apprentices enrolled in the Pennsylvania Institute School of Trades in November 1947, some of whom are shown in the photograph on page 169, were veterans. But hundreds of ex-GIs were unable to fit into even these expanded programs. Their desperate pleas helped persuade the state to open three temporary colleges for area students late in 1946. Martin and Rittenhouse Colleges used Philadelphia public school facilities for late afternoon and evening classes; Sproul College met at Chester High School.

Above, Philadelphians lining up in record numbers outside the city's Marriage License Bureau in May 1946 offered proof of the strong appeal of traditional family values for a war-weary population. The more than one thousand war brides who entered the city—mostly from Great Britain—similarly testified to the desire of veterans to resume normal home lives. In the photograph to the right, a 1948 class at the YWCA at 18th and Arch prepares war brides for citizenship exams. The postwar ideal returned women to the home and reemphasized their roles as wives and mothers. It led naturally to the baby boom of the 1940s and 1950s. The schools figured importantly in socializing teenage girls for their domestic responsibilities. To the far right, students at Southwest Philadelphia's John Bartram High School learn to tuck small children in for afternoon naps in April 1949.

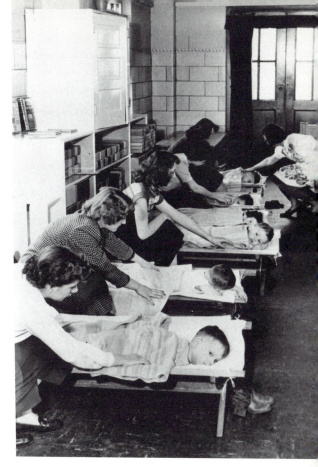

The postwar surge of purchasing power, which outstripped the supply of goods and services, led to inflation and shortages. Here, people line up in March 1946 for nylon stockings outside Edith Goldfarb Hosiery at 17th Street and Pacific in Tioga. Nylons had been on the market only a short time before the war curtailed their production. Cheaper and more durable than silk stockings and far superior to wartime substitutes made of rayon, nylon stockings were highly prized; enormous demand—even some small riots—greeted their renewed but limited availability in 1946. It was not till later in the year that the crisis subsided as manufacturers raised production and women discovered that they needed fewer of the longer-lasting nylons than they had of silk or rayon hosiery. Butter was also in short supply, but for a different reason. Wartime price controls remaining in effect limited the retail price of butter to 55 cents per pound, making it more profitable for suppliers to divert butterfat to other products. Butter was generally available only on the black market—at $1.80 per pound. On May 9, 1946, a farmers' cooperative tried to break the black market control of butter by selling the product at its legal price at the

Reading Terminal Market. Some of the twelve thousand customers who lined up to purchase butter—only four thousand were successful—are pictured on the next page. Note the cigar box in use as a cash drawer on the counter. By October, the crisis had worsened. The government had lifted controls, reimposing them when prices soared. Meat had virtually disappeared as suppliers held back their livestock.

Only part of the crowd at Reading Terminal's Pierce and Schurr stall trying to get lamb or veal appears in the photograph on the following page. The line stretched along 12th Street to Arch. In mid-October, President Harry Truman lifted price controls on meat; beef, lamb, and veal reappeared, but at predictably higher prices. By spring 1947, Truman was trying moral suasion to reverse the rapid rise in the cost

of living. Responding to the President's call, Marcus Bergsmann posed in April 1947 with customers of his delicatessen at 67th Avenue and Gratz Street in Oak Lane (page 175). Despite these efforts, the consumer price index in 1948 was one-third higher than it had been at war's end.

We Are Co-operating With PRES. TRUMAN'S REQUEST To Help Lower Cost of Living PRICES SLASHED 10%

Depression-era radicalism and the accumulated grievances of the no-strike war years carried over into a burst of postwar militance on the part of organized labor. Massive layoffs in mid-1945 reminded workers how uncertain their future was and further contributed to labor's aggressive stance. At an August 1945 rally (shown at the left) jointly sponsored by the American Federation of Labor and its rival, the Congress of Industrial Organization, more than twenty-five thousand workers assembled at Camden's Roosevelt Plaza to press for a continuation of the prolabor policies of the New Deal. Militance boiled over into strikes. Workers—many of them women hired during the war—march at the SKF Company at Front and Erie in late September 1945 (above). A spontaneous walkout by thirty-five workers protesting postwar layoffs led within a day to one thousand strikers ringing the plant. They were among the eighty thousand Philadelphians who struck in the four months after V-J Day.

MAGAZINES CIGARS GIFTS CANDIES PERFUMES DRUGS SODAS STATIONERY

178

The 1946 General Electric strike was reminiscent of the charged labor struggles of the 1930s. After mass picketing by five thousand electrical workers had closed the GE plant at 69th and Elmwood in Southwest Philadelphia for more than a month, the company obtained an anti-picketing injunction at the end of February. A clash between defiant picketers and a thousand Philadelphia police on February 27 led thirty-five hundred strikers and sympathizers to protest the next morning; hoisting an American flag (left), they marched down Woodland Avenue toward the plant. As they neared their goal, policemen on horses and motorcycles attacked. Police efforts to capture the flag (above), to deprive the strikers—many of them veterans—of their badge of Americanism, embittered the struggle. Labor organizations immediately began to organize a citywide protest of the police action, but Mayor Bernard Samuel arranged a truce. A week later, the nationwide United Electrical Workers walkout against General Electric ended in a victory for the strikers. The wave of strikes continued through 1946 in Philadelphia.

As they had during the Depression, popular protests spread out from the workplace into the neighborhoods; residents picketed, marched, and blockaded streets to call attention to local grievances. In the late 1940s, such demonstrations were more common in better-off white neighborhoods than in the poorer and older parts of the city. On the left, above, Hunting Park mothers block the intersection of Fifth and Cayuga to let their children cross safely in April 1948, one day after a car had killed a child there. A month later, residents of Ridgeway Street, near Rhawn, in Fox Chase, keep dirt-filled dump trucks off their street (opposite). In 1949, airborne pollution brought five hundred neighbors of South Philadelphia's Methodist Hospital out to complain about soot from the hospital's coal-fired boilers fouling the neighborhood.

Despite protests, strikes, and shortages, Philadelphians by and large
emerged from the war more prosperous than they had been for a
decade and a half; many were eager
to return to pleasures sometimes
curtailed by Depression and war.
Almost thirty-eight thousand fans
gathered at Shibe Park on April 17,
1946 to welcome Joe DiMaggio,
the Yankees, and peacetime baseball. A few days later, well-dressed
Easter Sunday crowds (opposite)
thronged Woodside Park, at Monu-
ment Avenue and Ford Road in
West Philadelphia, where they enjoyed rides, amusements, concerts,
and—by July, in a scene on the
next spread—swimming in Crystal
Pool.

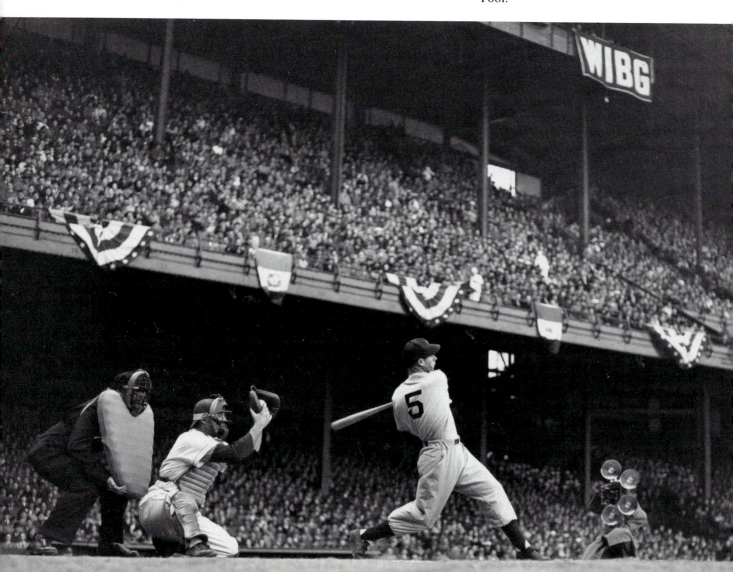

Residents of the city's rowhouse neighborhoods spent their leisure time in the late 1940s much as their parents had. On summer days, parents might bring children to neighborhood parks. Despite the debris cluttering the pond, Clark Park at 43rd and Chester in West Philadelphia looked inviting—certainly a comfortable alternative to houses without air conditioning—in the June 1947 photograph on the opposite page (top). Similarly, trash-strewn empty lots—like the one photographed (below) in 1947 at Bristol and Wayne in Tioga—remained, as they long had been, attractive play places for children willing to disregard their parents' warnings. The circus was also a part of leisure life in the city's older neighborhoods. The Ringling Brothers–Barnum & Bailey combined show set up in May 1947 at 11th and Erie for its first postwar visit to Philadelphia. The opening day crowd shown above included ten thousand children, most of whom were guests of restaurateur Frank Palumbo. Neighborhood residents set up stands along Erie Avenue to sell foods and trinkets to circus-goers.

By the end of the 1940s, the Cold War had spelled the end of the fevered climate of political radicalism and social criticism that had been a legacy of the Depression. Fearing Soviet Communism and domestic subversion, Americans determined to celebrate their institutions and silence their critics. The Cold War fostered such patriotic exercises as the Freedom Train, which started out from Philadelphia on September 17, 1947, taking 128 historic documents around the country. On the left, Philadelphians visit the train before its departure from 30th Street Station. Carrying the Constitution, the Declaration of Independence, and the Gettysburg Address, the train let parents instruct their children in the nation's traditions, as William Baker of Collingswood did (facing page, below) when the train stopped at the Camden Ferry Terminal in October 1948. When a federal court convicted twelve leaders of the once-influential American Communist Party on conspiracy charges one year later, protesters sympathetic to the defendants marched in front of the Federal Building at 9th and Market Streets, as illustrated below. Such open displays of radical sentiment would soon be virtually unknown.

The Enduring Rowhouse City

In the 1950s Philadelphia balanced between its immigrant and industrial past and its uncertain future in a suburbanized metropolis no longer dependent on the city for jobs, entertainment, shopping, or identity. Suburban growth and economic change transformed the city during that decade. Philadelphia remained very much a working-class community, but as the consumer society spread, even modest rowhouses began to fill with television sets, refrigerators, and electric appliances. Change came even to the rowhouse neighborhoods, but they remained the city's heart.

The old ways retained their vitality. Even the thousands of Philadelphians who moved into new developments in Roxborough, the Northeast, and Delaware County rarely severed their allegiances with the old neighborhoods quickly or entirely. Many Philadelphians relocated comfortably into semidetached houses or modern, spacious rowhouses resembling those they left behind. But their homage to the traditions their parents and grandparents had established in the city was obvious in the habits and attitudes they brought with them. They often moved into communities populated heavily by people just like their old neighbors. Many continued to shop in the old neighborhood. While rapid racial transition accompanied some of the population movements of the decade, most of the old white neighborhoods changed slowly in the 1950s, and residents who moved outward continued to be bound by ties of family and custom to those who stayed behind.

Most children and grandchildren of Philadelphia's immigrant communities still regarded the suburbs either as a dream, a home to more adventuresome or fortunate relatives and friends, or, more warily, as the abandonment of a familiar and meaningful world. They continued to live as their parents had, in rowhouses that stretched across the city's horizon. Over three-quarters of the city's houses were two-story brick rowhouses, and many of the rest differed only in their three-story height. They were old structures, dating mostly from the nineteenth century. In the most densely settled sections, between Lehigh and Oregon Avenues, thousands of families crowded into tightly packed streets and alleys, with as many as two hundred small houses on each block. These modest dwellings were comparatively inexpensive, allowing more Philadelphians to own their homes than rent. The rowhouse, then, did more than give the city its special texture; it increased the stake residents had in their communities, and also made those neighborhoods extraordinarily stable.

Ethnicity reinforced that stability. Relatively few Italians or Jews, the city's largest distinctive ethnic groups, lived in the suburbs. Italians remained concentrated in South Philadelphia, between 5th and 18th Streets, below Washington Avenue. By contrast, Jewish Philadelphians lived in several different neighborhoods, from Strawberry Mansion, West Oak Lane, and Oxford Circle north of the city center, to Wynnefield and Cobbs Creek in West Philadelphia, and below Mifflin east of Tenth Street in South Philadelphia. In these neighborhoods, as in such other communities as Polish Manayunk, ethnic ties bound families to each other and to their homes.

People also stayed in the old neighborhoods because these working-class districts held the factories and warehouses in which they worked. More than one in three Philadelphia jobs was in manufacturing when the decade began; textiles and metals accounted for half that employment. Several enormous firms—notably Budd with fourteen thousand workers and Philco with ten thousand —drew workers from across the city and suburbs, but most Philadelphians with industrial jobs worked for smaller, neighborhood-centered employers.

The factories, foundries, and mills that lined the railroads and riverbanks from Frankford Creek, Wingohocking Street, and Manayunk on the north, to Southwark and Gray's Ferry in South Philadelphia, explained the origins of the rowhouse communities. These industrial structures continued to cast their shadows over the neighborhoods, and Philadelphia retained its reputation as a city of small factories and skilled blue-collar workers. Plants producing chemicals, metals, and machinery lined the Delaware River waterfront north of Center City; sugar refineries, terminals, and warehouses stretched to the south. Metal-working shops and mills concentrated in Nicetown and along the Erie Avenue rail corridor. Oil refineries clustered along the lower Schuylkill. Loft buildings near downtown housed printshops, clothing manufacturers, and warehouses. And the remnants of a once-thriving textile industry persisted amid the decayed mill buildings of Manayunk, Kensington, and Frankford.

Industry had been the lifeblood of the rowhouse neighborhoods, their reason for being. But technological obsolescence and larger economic shifts took their toll among the older plants, and over the course of the decade the city lost fifty thousand, or one in seven, of its manufacturing jobs. The traditional industries of the city's older communities—textiles, clothing, machinery—lost more than their share. Only the city's extraordinarily diverse manufacturing base stemmed a more general decline. Employment actually rose in pharmaceuticals, electrical machinery, chemicals, and printing. The city's industrial patchwork unraveled somewhat, but different industries had distinct fates.

Philadelphia's overall loss of about seventy thousand of its two million people concealed a similar pattern. While the Northeast gained about a hundred thousand residents, the rest of the city that lay below Tacony Creek lost about one hundred and fifty thousand inhabitants—or 10 percent of its total. Here again the loss was uneven. The twin blights of population and job loss struck hardest in such older industrial neighborhoods as Kensington, Nicetown, Northern Liberties, and Southwark.

But even as the city was gradually losing population and industrial jobs, Philadelphia continued to attract blacks who found comparatively greater freedom and more opportunity here—often as unskilled laborers and service workers—than in the economically stagnant South. The black population grew by over a third during the decade. Numbering half a million by 1960, blacks were one-in-four of the city's residents.

Many of these newcomers moved into established black neighborhoods along South Street, in central North Philadelphia, and in West Philadelphia north of Market. Some settled in traditionally white factory districts, like Nicetown, Tioga, and parts of Germantown, which had been devastated by the loss of factory jobs. But even with declining populations and empty houses, most industrial neighborhoods resisted the black influx, their residents often fearful that black neighbors—like shuttered factories and the flight of white friends—spelled the end of their way of life. Ethnic and working-class Philadelphians shared the nation's prevailing racist culture; but in the city's industrial neighborhoods, continuing economic decline heightened tensions between the races during the decade.

It was in the streetcar suburbs built at the turn-of-the-century that blacks met the least resistance when they began to migrate. In these areas the racial composition of blocks and whole neighborhoods often changed entirely within a few years. Strawberry Mansion and Parkside most notably, and large areas of North and West Philadelphia in general, had not been interspersed with mills and factories. Some residents of the streetcar suburbs had been white-collar workers—clerks, retail employees, managers, professionals—in the years immediately after World War II; others were no better off financially than their fellow Philadelphians in the industrial neighborhoods. But the residents of the streetcar neighborhoods were alike in that they were not tied to their communities by factory and mill jobs. Those who shared more fully in the prosperity of the 1950s participated in the suburban exodus of the decade; the less well-to-do responded to the black influx by moving to other, still exclusively white parts of the city, often to the lower Northeast, the Olney–Oak Lane area, and Mount Airy. By 1960, there were three hundred and seventy-five thousand blacks in West Philadelphia above Baltimore Avenue and North Philadelphia below Lehigh. But there were fewer than ten thousand in all of Kensington, Frankford, Manayunk, Roxborough, and the Northeast combined.

Massive white flight from the old streetcar neighborhoods of North and West Philadelphia, white resistance to change in factory communities, and continued black migration from the South combined to make Philadelphia a city ever more divided by race in the 1950s. Race competed with ethnicity as the city's most salient social fact. While a third of all Philadelphians were still either immigrants or the children of immigrants and many lived in ethnically identifiable communities, blacks were more segregated from whites than any ethnic group had ever been from the city as a whole. Outsiders looking at Philadelphia in 1960 were likely to miss the city's rich ethnic mosaic and see instead a pattern drawn only in shades of white and black.

Many of the stately old houses visible just in front of the Cathedral of SS. Peter and Paul in the 1946 photograph of the 1600 block of Summer Street, at the top of the next page, had been transformed into apartments. Except for the fact that few people here owned their own homes, the texture of this neighborhood was typical of the densely packed old city in which most Philadelphians continued to live in the decade and a half following the war. The residents here were relatively poor, and virtually all were white, though no ethnic group predominated. Somewhat sur-prisingly in view of surrounding redevelopment projects and the lack of homeowners, this block survived more-or-less unchanged into the 1970s. About a mile away, the community around Marshall and Brown was part of the growing black area of North Philadelphia by the time the scene to the right was recorded in 1959. With its visibly deteriorated old rowhouses, only a few of which were owner occupied, and the racial uniformity evident in both the children—on their way to the Kearny Public School—and the adults, this community typified the segregated ghetto which now covered much of the old city.

Farther from the city's core, areas like Germantown and Manayunk continued to be remarkably self-sufficient. The 1951 view above of Conarroe Street in Manayunk illustrates the distinctive physical appearance of Philadelphia's most concentrated milltown. The spire of St. Mary's Church suggested an important aspect of life in this traditional community. But it was the mills and factories that supported Manayunk: on this block, a working brewery adjoined the church and its parochial school. Several of the larger plants along the canal were now abandoned, but others still produced the soap, textiles, and other goods whose manufacture had employed area residents for well over a century. Much of Germantown, in contrast, was a very middle-class residential area, though its stone mansions were interspersed with blocks of brick rowhouses as well. The working-class neighborhood around Lena and Earlham Streets, just east of historic Market Square, shown opposite and on the next page, was substantially Italian and had a growing black population when these photographs were taken in 1950. Though there were factories nearby, the images in both photographs of people washing their cars and children riding bicycles on neat, tree-lined streets convey the attractions Germantown offered successive waves of newcomers fleeing the industrial rowhouse neighborhoods of the old city.

Shopping areas—sometimes no more than a few stores, occasionally a major commercial avenue—often gave neighborhoods their sense of identity. The 1947 scene below at the corner of 58th Street and Florence, near the western edge of the city below Baltimore Avenue, with its combination of small shops and eateries, was typical of one kind of white, middle-class trolleycar neighborhood. Though clearly urban, this was a community at some remove from the city's worst problems. Depicted on the following page, in 1951, is the busy intersection of Midvale and Ridge Avenues in East Falls, which was even more self-contained. Yet many of the ten thousand residents of East Falls did their major shopping neither in their own neighborhood nor in downtown Philadelphia. Instead, they took a trolley up Midvale to the great regional shopping area at Germantown and Chelten Avenues. The view on page 201, taken for the Germantown Community Council around 1960, is along Germantown Avenue toward the Germantown Savings Bank sign at School House Lane. Rowell's and Allen's department stores, the Vernon Theater, banks, and specialty shops made this a magnet for the hundreds of thousands of people in northwest Philadelphia and the nearby suburbs. By 1960, old regional centers like this were vulnerable to the shift of middle-class population to the suburbs and the growth of the more automobile-accessible shopping centers located farther out of the city.

Outdoor markets and pushcart vendors remained part of the fabric of daily life in the older neighborhoods. These photographs of women examining pots and dresses at the 9th Street Italian market illustrate both the variety of goods available and the persistence of Philadelphia's most famous market street. Yet there had been changes on the six blocks between Christian and Wharton Streets from the time the first photograph was taken in 1947 and the second in 1959. After a long fight, the city had managed to end the sale of meat, poultry, fish, and cheese from pushcarts, limiting the latter to dry goods, fruits, and vegetables. Like most of the city's other outdoor markets, the old Marshall Street Jewish market, home to hundreds of pushcart peddlers from early in the century, was in decline. When the photographs on the next spread were taken in 1960, only about a dozen pushcart operators remained. Lillian Agard cleans a head of lettuce at a stand she and her husband Sam had operated since 1923. Nearby, Morris Mondoil, whose father Harry had become known as the "Greeney Millionaire" by selling stringbeans, still sold them.

Other scenes could still evoke memories of older habits and a more slow-paced life. Above, left, a black shoeshine man plies his trade in the 1950s in Reyburn Plaza, later the site of the Municipal Services Building. Left, junkmen and rag collectors still made their rounds with horse-drawn wagons as late as 1949. The small-town, almost rustic general store above had been at Rhawn and Loretto in Northeast Philadelphia since Rhawnhurst had started to develop in the 1920s. By 1949 it was unusual enough to attract the attention of a city photographer. At the other end of the city, Stone House Lane, northeast of the Navy Yard between Packer and Pattison, was still the site of a squatters' shantytown in 1955. About two hundred people lived here on the site of abandoned pig farms in the area long known as "The Neck." Most, like William Evert, raised chickens and goats as the photograph on the next page documents. But the days of this shantytown were coming to an end. As part of the city's downtown redevelopment, the Dock Street food complex was to be relocated here in a new Food Distribution Center, and by 1956, the last squatters had been evicted.

Urban planners hoping to improve life in the city's poor districts advocated comprehensive urban renewal programs, arguing that these would transform entire neighborhoods as well as the lives of those moving into decent housing in new communities. But relatively few areas underwent comprehensive renewal. North Philadelphia's East Poplar area was a notable exception. The 1950 view below of 8th and Brown in East Poplar shows the crowded, unhealthy conditions that had plagued this area since the turn of the century. This block was transformed by 1952 into the Friends Housing Cooperative, a one-hundred-unit project intended as a model for interracial and cooperative living. The East Poplar Urban Renewal Area, which combined the efforts of public agencies, private investors, and local groups like the Friends Neighborhood Guild, was in many ways an exception to the overall failure of neighborhood urban renewal. Its example was not followed elsewhere in North Philadelphia.

Public housing was a far more common government response to the city's poor. The more than five thousand homes and apartments built during the 1950s—far less than the number reformers hoped for—made this the decade of massive projects and ill-fated high-rises so out of character for Philadelphia. As in the 1930s, public housing was intended for working-class families who would someday buy their own houses, but the projects rarely seemed to work out as waystations on the road out of poverty. Because limited funding canceled many of the planned amenities, the projects were generally bleak; because public housing could not challenge racial segregation, projects for blacks were built only in poor black areas of North and South Philadelphia. In addition, clearing the land for housing and renewal projects actually destroyed more homes than were built, and relocation shredded the fragile fabric of many communities. But many regarded public housing as a considerable improvement over the slums it usually replaced. The vision of

public housing as an instrument for social uplift is clearly expressed in these photographs. The predominately white Tasker Homes, shown on the next page, top, were built at 31st and Morris in South Philadelphia in 1943 originally for war workers. A group of tenants at the Richard Allen Homes on 12th Street above Fairmount in 1953 is shown on the same page. The Housing Association of the Delaware Valley took both photographs to illustrate positive solutions to the city's problem of aging housing. Such apparently successful rowhouse projects were succeeded by large high-rise projects based in part on European models. On page 211, residents sit in front of the eleven-story, high-rise Norris Homes, which opened in 1954 at 11th and Norris in North Philadelphia. Many similar and even larger structures were erected in Philadelphia's older neighborhoods throughout the decade. The later, troubled history of public housing is not visible in these idealized and genuinely hopeful scenes from the 1950s.

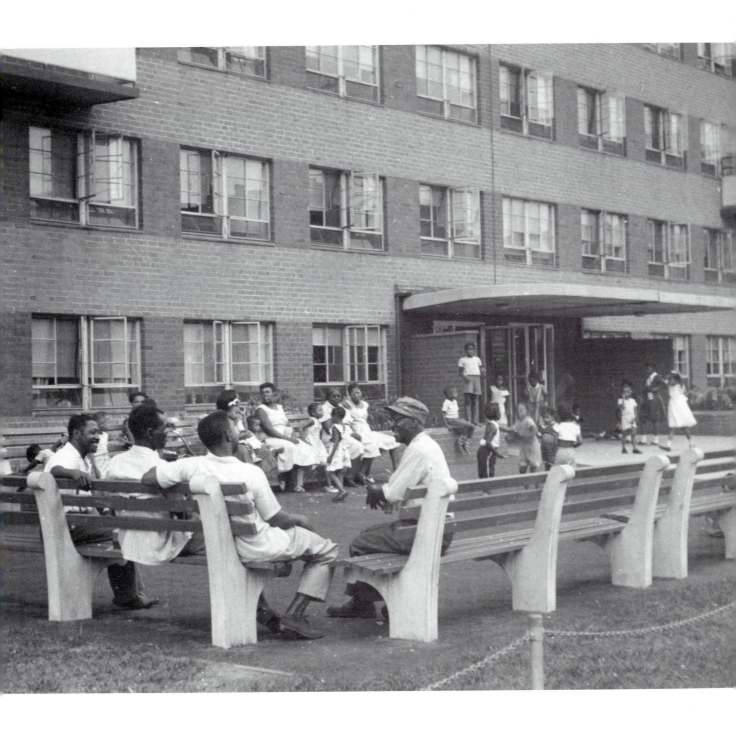

Race transformed the old city more than any other force in the 1950s. An increasing black population, a declining white population, and the persistence of *de facto* segregation turned most of North Philadelphia below Lehigh Avenue into a ghetto. Three in ten of the area's residents in 1940 had been black; by 1960, the proportion was seven in ten. Outsiders driving through North Philadelphia on Broad Street rarely saw the rich tapestry of working-class and middle-class communities; nor did they generally recognize the important sociability of street life. This is the 1200 block of North Hutchinson Street, between 9th and 10th, just above Girard. The Housing Association used the image on the next page to show a typical though unnamed street in a published study of Central North Philadelphia. Both photographs provide glimpses of community life, rather than overly dramatized problems or carefully presented solutions. But the area did have its share of problems, and the Housing Association photographed them as it had been documenting similar situations in the city's poorer communities since the beginning of the century. The photograph at the top of page 215 shows Chris Johnson in his cellar room at 1530 North Marvine, between 11th and 12th below Oxford, in the spring of 1957, after an urban renewal project had forced him out of his previous home. Below are Mrs. Payton and her son Robert Lee in another apartment on the same block. Both homes eventually fell to urban renewal bulldozers.

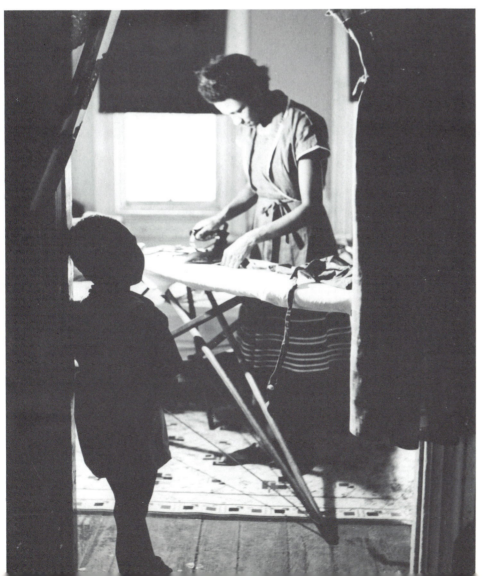

Despite the city's continuing industrial decline, manufacturing in 1960 still employed more Philadelphians than the service sector. The American Street industrial corridor (seen at the left in a late 1940s southward aerial view at its intersection with Lehigh Avenue) suggested both the strengths and the weaknesses of the city's economy. Straddling the railroad tracks, which served as the lifeline for many of the old plants, are metalworking plants, textile mills, and food-processing operations. These factories employed residents of nearby rowhouses and thousands of others within easy walking distance from other parts of Kensington. But the antiquated buildings and the absence of space for expansion did not bode well for the long-term future. Nicetown, to the west, also owed its existence to railroads industry. At left is the massive Midvale Steel Works in 1951; it had been located at Wissahickon and Roberts since 1867. Midvale's twenty-three hundred employees did precision steel work in forty buildings spread over seventy acres. Other plants producing automotive parts and transmission equipment made Nicetown the city's most important center of traditional heavy industry. Just outside Philadelphia, the Baldwin Locomotive Works at Eddystone covered nearly a square mile and employed seven thousand workers when this photograph (right) of men guiding the subassembly of a locomotive cab was taken in 1950. Over the decades, these and other industries had created a formidable and diversified skilled workforce and specialized physical plants that would not easily or quickly disappear.

Thousands of Philadelphians worked in smaller industrial and service enterprises. The workers shown above, inspecting bread on the way to the wrapper at the Freihofer Bakery at 20th and Indiana in 1946, were among the eleven thousand employed in the city's one hundred and thirty bakeries. But bakeries could suffer obsolescence just as steel mills, and Freihofer's sold this building in 1958. The city's large food industry workforce in 1950 also included Dolores Haley, Yetta Pesco, and Betha Blatt, on the facing page, sorting and capping strawberries—presumably before the berries were dipped in chocolate at Abbott's Dairies at 3rd and Lombard. The city was home to many specialty trades; a 1950 *Evening Bulletin* feature on workplaces in the lofts around City Hall depicted Mollie Porrini and Phyllis Zanan of West Philadelphia and Gilda Palamone of South Philadelphia turning out athletic equipment for juveniles on the fourth floor of 1307 Cuthbert Street (page 220). That many of these workers were women is not surprising. In 1950, women were nearly a third of the city's workforce, and a third of all shop-floor factory workers. Blacks also found positions in many industries, though they faced job ceilings in many areas if they tried to advance. Depicted (on page 221) are construction workers in a street crew at 6th and Market in 1958. Blacks expanded their presence in construction work as laborers when these jobs became less attractive to whites, especially Italians, who were moving on to better work. By 1960, over half of all laborers locally were black, statistical evidence of the employment discrimination that limited most blacks to positions at the bottom of the workforce.

221

Newer industries—electronics, electrical machinery, and consumer appliances—contributed more than their share to Philadelphia's economy in the 1950s. By decade's end, electrical machinery manufacture—with over thirty thousand workers—was the city's third largest industry. The computer age had dawned in Philadelphia; scientists and engineers at the University of Pennsylvania had developed ENIAC during World War II. Univac was a consequence of that effort; non-existent in 1948, that computer company had more than fourteen hundred employ-

ees locally by 1958. The area was also an early center of the television industry; specialized suppliers developed here alongside such industry giants as RCA. Above, Jerrold Electronics, at 15th and Lehigh about 1960, was the world's largest manufacturer of amplified antenna systems to bring television to remote areas. Its founder, future Governor Milton Shapp, had pleased city officials when he decided in 1958 to keep his booming business in North Philadelphia. Workers at Philco build refrigerators in 1950, opposite page, at the company's huge plant—the former Atwater Kent Company—at 4700 Wissahickon Avenue. Philco, despite a decline in its city workforce from nearly fourteen thousand in 1948 to eight thousand in 1958, was for many years the city's largest peacetime employer.

From the production of long rifles in the early years of the new nation, the Philadelphia area had been a center of military manufacture. The emergence of the "military-industrial complex" in the 1950s did not favor this region's economy as fully as it did that of the South and West, but Korean War and Cold War defense spending did influence the local economy. The hulls and turrets of Patton tanks rolling along the assembly line at the Budd plant in 1952, as shown here, contributed to Budd's position as the area's largest industrial employer during the Korean conflict. The Navy Yard also flourished, employing more than fourteen thousand, six hundred workers in 1952. By the time the photograph on the next page was taken in 1959, employment at the yard had dropped to just under ten thousand, and city politicians were scurrying to Washington to save local jobs. The eleven thousand employees at Camden's New York Shipbuilding Company were working in 1959 on about $200 million in Navy contracts. On page 227, workers at New York Shipbuilding move a 125-ton nuclear reactor into the *Savannah*, the world's first nuclear-powered freighter. In 1959, when Philadelphia-area firms won $690 million in new government contracts, about forty-four thousand civilian workers, or one-twelfth of the area workforce, were employed on government contracts. From Philco's new Sidewinder missile, to Vertol's aircraft and Burroughs' defense warning system, Philadelphia-area companies capitalized on the area's traditional industries and skills—and its new strength in electronics—to take advantage of the Cold War threats that formed the dark side of the 1950s.

Family Album, 1945–1960

A group of friends shortly after V-J Day in 1945. The young man in the army uniform on the left is Maurice Kashi; he has just returned from Germany. The man on the right is in the Merchant Marine and has just come off a tanker. The young woman and the children are neighbors. This photograph was taken in the 2700 block of South Randolph Street between Johnston and Oregon Avenues.

Verna Phillips collecting from Gordon Johnson for the Easter Seals anti-tuberculosis campaign in the late 1940s. The widespread voluntary campaigns against polio (the March of Dimes) and tuberculosis diminished along with the threats from those diseases in the 1960s, when cancer and heart disease took center stage in charitable fund-raising.

The Kensington High School Senior Prom held at the Broadwood Hotel, Broad and Wood Streets May 12, 1945. The war in Europe had ended just four days before, adding joy to the festive occasion, but there was still a shortage of men. Many of the young women had boyfriends but they were in the service. To make up for the shortage, the prom committee invited extra men from Girard College and they were assigned dates by height. Nen Wagner, the girl at the extreme right of the photograph, cannot even remember the name of her date. This was the last time she ever saw him.

Four generations of the Shipman family at a picnic in Hunting Park on the Fourth of July 1946. Even with the end of wartime gasoline rationing, many families stayed close to home for holidays.

Four loyal football fans from Northeast Catholic High School in the fall of 1951 after a football game between Northeast Catholic and Lincoln high schools. In the back row of this picture, taken in the Mayfair section of Northeast Philadelphia, are Barbara Lyons and Ginnie MacGregor. In the front are Mildred De Blasio and Esther Lyons. Note the long skirts, the hair styles, and the sweaters.

Bride and groom slicing the cake at a home wedding reception, probably in the early 1950s. This photograph is one of thousands by John W. Mosley, who documented life in Philadelphia's black communities from 1937 to 1967.

Samuel Brooks standing proudly beside his new 1953 Oldsmobile Delta 88, the first model to have power brakes and directional signals on the steering wheel. Many American families have similar snapshots—Americans have never been able to resist taking a photograph of the new car.

During the Korean War, as in World War II, a great many servicemen and women came to Philadelphia on weekend passes. With Fort Dix, McGuire Air Force Base, and the Navy Yard nearby, the city was a favorite place to spend a few hours or days. The USO and the Salvation Army, as well as many churches and clubs, tried to provide wholesome entertainment for these servicemen and women and thereby to keep them away from other more "dangerous" activities. This is a photograph of a black social club in the early 1950s. Notice the length of the women's skirts and the "Ike Jackets," the Army dress uniform of the Korean War era.

A Memorial Day parade in 1952. The Korean War increased the importance of patriotic displays on such occasions. The Girl Scout and Brownie Troops sponsored by the First Presbyterian Church of Holmesburg are marching north on the 8500 block of Frankford Avenue. Saint Dominic's Church and Cemetery are in the background. Joanne Gargani, who preserved the photograph, is carrying the flag.

A family portrait taken in December 1955 at 2047 South 67th Street in Southwest Philadelphia, on the occasion of Thomas J. Curry, Jr.'s first visit home after Air Force basic training. Even though the Korean War ended in 1953, young men continued to be drafted and others joined the Armed Forces. Just as in World War II, returning serviceman provided a photo opportunity and a symbolic occasion to record the entire family together. Seated on the couch are Sarah Curry, Thomas J. Curry, Sr., and Thomas J. Curry, Jr. On the floor are Mary Grace Curry with her doll and Michael Curry.

Two young Philadelphians, dressed in the latest style, relax on the boardwalk in Wildwood, New Jersey, in the summer of 1953.

Another mock wedding, this one celebrates a twenty-fifth wedding anniversary. The woman in the gown on the left and the man next to her are the guests of honor in 1952 or 1953, as neighbors from the 2800 block of East Venango restage the original event. Note the shotgun.

Children on the porch at 5868 North 6th Street all set to go "trick-or-treating" on Halloween 1953.

Mr. and Mrs. Thomas Bentz, with their two children, all dressed in their Sunday best, pose in the backyard of 4476 Salmon Street in the spring of 1954. Notice the playhouses and the pigeon coops. Raising pigeons remained a favorite hobby in the Bridesburg section of the city in the early 1950s. Except for the clothes, this picture could have been taken twenty-five—or even fifty—years earlier.

Barbara Klaczynska, her mother Helen, and Sister
Mary Celine in the schoolyard of St. Adalbert's,
in Port Richmond, after Barbara's First Holy
Communion in May 1955.

Michael, John, and Mary Branigan playing in the rear of 2206
Stanwood Street in Northeast Philadelphia in the late fall of
1956. Note that the little girl is wearing a dress and carrying a
doll, while her brothers wear pants and carry guns. That is a
1954 Plymouth in the driveway.

Almost every family has a collection of school photographs. A class of wiggling youngsters suddenly becomes still for an instant as they say "cheese" for the photographer and the image is preserved for all time. This is Miss Bailey's first grade class at the Henry H. Houston School, in Mount Airy, in October 1955.

People took photographs of their businesses as well as of their children and cars. This is a neighborhood store run by Aram and Siranoush Aghazarian about 1955. The business was at 3922 Fairmount Avenue in a largely black neighborhood; the owners lived in an apartment above the store. The store was open twelve hours a day, six days a week, and from 8 AM to 1 PM on Sunday. The occasion for this photograph was probably a prize won by Cliff, a salesman who stands to the right.

Elin and Charles Pitkapaasi in front of their house at 4118 West Girard Avenue in 1958. The neighborhood was in transition from Jewish to black at this time, but there was still a large Jewish delicatessen between 40th and 41st Streets. There were also a theater, a bakery, a bar, and two drug stores. The Pitkapaasi family remembers buying huge corned beef sandwiches at the deli or at the Brass Rail Restaurant and carrying them one block away to Fairmount Park for picnics.

Dellie Werner Rosen at her home in Northeast Philadelphia in May 1959, getting ready to go to the prom at the Philadelphia College of Pharmacy. Note the strapless gown, the corsage pinned at the waist, and the wonderful lamp at the right.

Metropolis Reshaped

The varied experiences of Depression, war, and peacetime reconversion had at least one common aspect: the period from the early 1930s through the late 1940s saw little new residential or commercial construction. Philadelphia stagnated. With few exceptions, the buildings and the neighborhoods of 1950 differed from those of 1930 only in being twenty years older. As the war receded, Philadelphians returned to the unfinished agenda of the 1920s, rebuilding their city and their region to take advantage of the possibilities unleashed by new technologies. The suburban growth of the 1920s resumed, as did the reconstruction of the city center. The decade of the 1950s differed from the city's last period of sustained growth in being based on a more widespread—though by no means complete —prosperity and thus in offering new homes and new neighborhoods to more Philadelphians. A new city—more spread out, more divided, more obviously wealthy, and more desperately poor—appeared in the 1950s.

A new split-level house or a "colonial" bungalow with a manicured lawn and newly planted trees symbolized the triumph of the suburb as an American ideal. Philadelphians by the tens of thousands made this dream a reality in the 1950s, shifting the region's population center from city to suburb. The census of 1960 was the first to locate more area residents in the seven outlying counties than in the city. The population of the suburban ring grew by 700,000 to 2,300,000 during the decade; only the growth of the essentially suburban Northeast by 200,000 to 300,000 in the same period kept the city from actually declining in population.

Suburbs in lower Montgomery, eastern Delaware, and lower Bucks Counties grew fastest, with the latter area nearly tripling in population. Most of the growth came from Philadelphians abandoning their city neighborhoods and from the high birth rate among young suburban families. In some areas, like Cherry Hill and the Northeast, development marched across a broad front from existing residential neighborhoods, transforming farmland or similarly underused parcels of real estate in a steady block-by-block advance. Elsewhere, fingers of development stretching out along highways and commuter railroads lengthened and thickened. This was the case with the suburban corridors extending toward Hatboro and Paoli. Only rarely in the 1950s did developers gamble on dropping entirely new communities into settings isolated from adjacent development, though Levittown and Fairless Hills—both in Bucks County—were prominent exceptions.

Automobiles and affordable houses—brought within reach of many Philadelphians by wartime savings, postwar prosperity, and a series of government programs—stimulated suburbanization. The 1950s saw a national infatuation with the car—with its styling, power, and accessories; that interest was focused most strongly in the suburbs, where automobile ownership became nearly universal over the course of the decade. By 1960, there were 120 cars for every 100 families in the Philadelphia suburbs, while every 100 city families owned only 67 cars. Massive highway projects—the two state turnpikes, the Schuylkill Expressway, and the upgrading of dozens of state highways—made the advent of the suburban automobile age possible.

A quarter-million new houses—many financed by subsidized Veterans' Administration and Federal Housing Administration mortgages—appeared in the Philadelphia suburbs in the 1950s. Favoring new construction rather than the renovation of older structures in order to stimulate the economy, the government programs enabled tens of thousands of area families to buy ranch and split-level houses surrounded by lawns and yards unavailable in the city. Residential developments sprawled across the landscape, with each unit of suburban housing using land enough, on average, for seven city houses.

The suburbs of the 1950s were meant to be residential preserves, domestic retreats isolated from the bustle, decay, and economic activity of the city. The main exceptions were preexisting and increasingly invisible factory towns like Camden, Chester, Norristown, and Conshohocken, some new industrial parks, and a steadily growing number of shopping centers. Though the origins of the shopping center date back to the 1920s, it was only after the war that automobile-oriented centers under a single management and with a targeted set of tenants became common. Dozens of centers, like Ellisburg Circle in New Jersey, combined retail and convenience stores with a large supermarket near a busy highway intersection. But in the conservative business climate of Philadelphia, few large department stores followed the rush to the suburbs as their counterparts did in other cities. Only near the end of the decade did Lit Brothers and Gimbels venture as far afield as Northeast Philadelphia.

Industries speeded up their one-hundred-year history of suburbanization, moving now into new industrial parks rather than the decaying cores of the old factory towns lining the region's rivers. Located on spacious grounds away from residential neighborhoods, industrial parks appeared throughout the metropolitan area. King of Prussia attracted SKF, General Electric, Burroughs, and Sharp and Dohme; Ford and Pepsi Cola moved into Pennsuaken. The most important new industrial plant in the region was United States Steel's massive Fairless Works—with six thousand employees—in lower Bucks County. But jobs were slower to leave the city than people. In the late 1950s, almost two-thirds of regional employment was in Philadelphia, and about one hundred and twenty-seven thousand wage earners commuted from suburban homes to city jobs.

With industry relatively out of sight and single-family subdivisions nearly ubiquitous, the suburbs had a homogeneous appearance. Contributing to their look were their residents—mostly white, middle-class, young families. And almost everywhere there were children, the citizens for whom the safe retreat of suburban life seemed to have been designed. Philadelphia's aging population managed to add only 65,000 children in the decade; the less populous but younger suburbs grew by 332,000 children in the same period.

Equally striking were differences in education, income, and race. The 1960 census showed that most adult suburbanites had completed high school; in Philadelphia the comparable number was one-third. Education was a central concern of the youth-oriented suburbs, of which lavish new schools were as characteristic as shopping centers. Further, most new developments targeted the middle- or upper-middle classes; by the late 1950s, average annual family income in Montgomery and Delaware Counties was $8,000, compared to $6,500 in the city. The historic pockets of poverty in the old industrial towns and in some of the rural communities were increasingly out of place in the suburban counties.

The suburbs were far from homogeneous despite appearances. Sometimes subtle restrictions on the immigrants and the children of immigrants who made it to the suburbs in the 1950s led them to be less than completely welcome in some communities. The percentage of foreign-born in the suburban counties as a whole nearly equaled that of the city. But informal real estate practices like steering prospective buyers where they would be comfortable—and until the 1960s legally binding restrictive covenants—meant that some suburban communities would have very few Jews or Italians, and others consequently would have more. Italians concentrated in lower Bucks and Camden Counties and in Upper Darby. The Camden suburbs and lower Montgomery County had large Jewish populations, though the major Jewish migration was to Northeast Philadelphia. It

Fairless
Hills

B U C K S

Levittown

611

Hatboro

Ambler

M O N T G O M E R Y

232

73

Turnpike

Abington

202

Pennsylvania

1

422

Norristown

309

Jenkintown

Springfield
Twp.

Cheltenham

130

King of
Prussia

Conshohocken

23

73

B U R L I N G T O N

422

Radnor

Palmyra

Moorestown

Paoli

Wayne

Villanova

Bryn Mawr

73

Lower
Merion

C H E S T E R

Ardmore

Bala
Cynwyd

38

320

Haverford

PHILADELPHIA

Newton
Square

Benjamin
Franklin
Bridge

Pennsauken

Upper
Darby

Camden

Cherry
Hill

252

1

Drexel Hill

Yeadon

70

D E L A W A R E

Lansdowne
Clifton
Hts.

Aldan

Collings-
dale

Collingswood

Haddonfield

Media

Springfield

Ridley

76

Swarth-
more

Sharon Hill

Walt
Whitman
Bridge

C A M D E N

73

Delaware

River

42

Chester

Woodbury

41

30

130

G L O U C E S T E R

New Jersey Turnpike

++++++ Pennsylvania, Reading, and Pennsylvania-Reading Seashore Railroads

244

was not until the Schuylkill Expressway expanded settlement along the farther reaches of the Main Line, leaving houses in Bala Cynwyd and Merion Station in need of buyers, that Jews were able to gain significant entry to the Main Line.

But the greatest segregation was by race. Blacks increased to one-quarter of Philadelphia's population; in the suburban counties the black proportion—mostly relegated to the decaying industrial towns in any case—fell slightly during the 1950s to 6.1 percent. An immense racial gap opened between the city and the suburbs. Few bothered to hide housing segregation practices. Developers and realtors presented neighborhoods like the Northeast as white preserves. With the exception of the industrial towns and small historic enclaves in LaMott and along the Main Line, the suburbs were quite white. Montgomery County's half-million residents included only eighteen thousand blacks in 1960.

Some contemporaries labeled the migration to the suburbs "white flight." Paralleling that movement—and compounding the injustice to those left behind because of race—was the transformation of the regional economy. The city lost sixty thousand blue-collar and craft jobs in the 1950s—a figure matched by the gain in comparable positions in the suburbs, where many of the jobs were inaccessible to Philadelphia blacks. Equally troubling for the city was a shift in white-collar employment. Though Philadelphia maintained a disproportionate share of the region's offices, the city lost about twenty thousand managerial jobs to the suburbs. And the city's net increase of fifteen thousand clerical, professional, technical, and sales jobs paled next to the suburban gain of one hundred and twenty thousand such positions. These trends threatened Philadelphia's historic role at the center of the regional economy.

The threat especially disturbed the city's business community, which had invested heavily in downtown Philadelphia. Beginning in the mid-1940s, business leaders spearheaded efforts to reinvigorate the city by rebuilding its core. Using newly granted powers to seize land for nongovernmental purposes, Philadelphia's corporate and political leaders began to create high-income residential developments and to build more office towers of the sort begun in the 1920s. Indeed, the "Renaissance," as the renewal effort and its associated political movement was called, was very much limited in its vision to the unfinished agenda of the 1920s and to the problems of that earlier time. The city's leaders decided to compete with the suburbs for the upscale white residents whose outward movement had surged dramatically in the 1920s; but the city's leadership responded only minimally to the central issue of postwar Philadelphia—the flight of jobs, especially industrial positions, to the suburbs. The enduring tragedy of the Renaissance was its deliberate destruction of the livelihoods and homes of many working-class Philadelphians.

  The most notable successes of the center city renewal were the malls framing Independence Hall, the replacement of the Pennsylvania Railroad tracks west of City Hall and the "Chinese Wall" with the uninspired blocks of Penn Center, the residential development of the Parkway, and, especially, Society Hill. Colonial standards of scale and design influenced the Society Hill project. But the rebuilding of the older city was no more a return to Philadelphia's roots than the antiseptic stage set of Colonial Williamsburg was a revival of early Virginia. Planners and investors meant the neighborhood to be distinctively residential and upper class, not the messy and vital hodgepodge of trade, crafts, and residences—rich and poor—that marked the colonial city when it was the commercial capital of the new world.

Downtown Philadelphia appeared after the war much as it had when the Depression had taken hold a generation earlier. Almost a quarter of a million people came to work every day in the central city between Vine and South Streets and the two rivers; theaters, restaurants, and three thousand retail shops drew another hundred and fifty thousand people downtown on an average day. To the right, Christmas shoppers throng Market Street around 12th in 1948. But as the photographs on the following spread demonstrate, the downtown also had conspicuous problems. The inefficient and even unhealthy Dock Street Market, next to the Delaware River below Walnut Street, was in a belt of antiquated warehouses and obsolescent industrial buildings that strangled the eastern third of the downtown, and the "Chinese Wall," the local name for the Pennsylvania Railroad elevated tracks along Market Street west of Broad Street Station, choked the downtown from the west until its removal in 1952.

249

After a wartime surge of patriotism had focused attention on Independence Hall as an icon of America's national identity, a group of prominent local citizens involved the federal and state governments in creating a historic park as a setting for that shrine. From its outset, the project was also meant to stop the southward spread of the city's skid-row district and to anchor the redevelopment of the eastern part of the city core as a modern business district and a wealthy residential neighborhood. Redevel-opment capitalized on the area's colonial and early national history, but ignored the important Victorian residential and commercial buildings. In replacing structures planners considered obsolete and land uses they thought inappropriate, redevelopers destroyed over a century of the city's recent history and the homes and livelihoods of many downtown residents. To the left, above, an elevated view shows mid- and late-nineteenth-century commercial buildings north of Independence Hall in the late 1940s.

A closer view below looks west along the 500 block of Market Street in November 1950. Early phases of the Independence Mall project (above, in 1957) left much of the varied district of loft industries, warehouses, discount stores, and wholesalers intact.

251

The 1951 election of reform Mayor Joseph Clark brought to power urban planners and corporate leaders committed to reviving the downtown as the focus of a new white-collar economy. Near the heart of their strategy was the conversion of Society Hill, one of the city's poorest and most dilapidated districts, into a wealthy residential community. Public funds underwrote land clearance and rehabilitation in the blocks between Walnut and Lombard east of 6th Street. The neighborhood's early history and its colonial- and early national-era houses also attracted well-to-do families—some of them suburbanites—to rehabilitate and move into houses then gaining popularity, in part because of a growing interest in all things "colonial." Here Mr. and Mrs. Earle Kirkbride strike a pose scraping away paint and wallpaper from one of the three fireplaces at their Front Street home in 1956. On the right are restored houses on the 200 block of Pine Street in the same year. A dramatic rise in property values testified to the success of the Society Hill project. Population fell by half as multiple-occupancy rental housing gave way to homeowning families.

Penn Center—which occupied the site of the Chinese Wall that the Pennsylvania Railroad began to demolish in 1952—was the commercial counterpart of Society Hill. The original plans for the area along the north side of Market Street from 15th to 18th Streets called for office towers separated by large plazas. Economic considerations soon scaled back the open space. The first Penn Center building was constructed in 1954 and 1955, and the cleared site of the two buildings which followed in 1957 is visible in the photograph to the left. Though Penn Center was an architectural failure, these were the first office buildings built downtown since the Depression and they did help keep office jobs in the city. Immediately to the northwest, between 22nd and 24th along the south side of the Parkway, the North Triangle residential project suffered because the slow progress of Penn Center kept the area isolated from the rest of the downtown. The four luxury apartment buildings of Park Towne Place ultimately replaced the businesses, warehouses, and houses under demolition in the 1958 scene below.

The continuing expansion of the metropolitan area broke down the relative autonomy of several old market towns, turning established communities near Philadelphia into upper-middle-class bedroom communities. An aerial view of Jenkintown, in Montgomery County, in 1951 is shown to the left. Running diagonally across the scene is Old York Road, with the main shopping district on the left near West Avenue, and Strawbridge & Clothier, one of the few prewar suburban branches of a center-city department store, in the lower right. Also visible are the homes of many of the borough's five thousand residents and—in the distance—the neighboring town of Cheltenham. Jenkintown was nine miles north of central Philadelphia; dozens of trains made the twenty-minute trip daily. Haddonfield, New Jersey—seven miles east of downtown Philadelphia—was, like Jenkintown, a Quaker settlement dating from around 1700. The community's well-preserved old shopping district stretches along Kings Highway (above). A bedroom suburb for many of Camden's executives and professionals, Haddonfield had no factories or rowhouses. This 1949 image suggests the small-town self-sufficiency beloved by local residents. But modern transportation and the growth of managerial jobs had provided towns like Haddonfield and Jenkintown with specific roles in the metropolitan community.

A complex web of trains, trolleys, bus lines, and highways tied the metropolis together, providing Philadelphia with a much better public transportation system than most American cities. About a hundred thousand commuters from adjacent Pennsylvania counties used the system to enter the city daily. The 69th Street Terminal in Upper Darby—a major hub of this system—shifted suburbanites from their automobiles or from the Red Arrow system to the Market Street Subway-Elevated for a quick ride to the city center. Above, a trolley makes its way down the center of State Street in Media toward 69th Street in 1950. Opposite, cars park along the busy 6800 block of Market Street across from the Philadelphia Transit Company parking lot in 1947. The area around the PTC–Red Arrow Terminal had grown into one of Delaware County's major shopping districts, with such stores as Gimbels, Lits, and Arnold Constable, dozens of lesser concerns, and several large theaters. With the consolidation of the Red Arrow system, the suburban transit company had rebuilt its part of the old terminal in 1936. On page 260, commuters wait at the terminal in 1948 to board the Red Arrow Sharon Hill line, which carried well over ten thousand riders a day in the late 1940s and served the expanding eastern Delaware County communities of Drexel Hill, Clifton Heights, and Aldan. Though they still worked in the city, these obviously prosperous office workers and professionals were the kind of people the city had already lost to the suburbs before the great exodus of the 1950s.

Much of the new construction in the city's Northeast merely added a suburban gloss to traditional row-house design. The thousands of Korman and Orleans houses in those new neighborhoods made as little provision for preserving open space as zoning regulations required in the city's older sections. An official city photographer recorded the scene around Hellerman and Farnsworth, above, one block east of Roosevelt Boulevard in the center of postwar development, in September 1950. Just as their predecessors had done half a century earlier, developers were able to squeeze 96 two-story houses—each on a lot about 20 by 100 feet—onto a city block. In the 1951 photograph on the next page, the Philadelphia *Bulletin* captured residents of the 6100 block of Shisler Street (just below Devereaux) tending their lawns in a new community where a home-owners' club promoted sociability. Only a block and a half to the east, Castor Avenue (looking north from Levick) had been transformed in the few years since the war into a major shopping strip; in 1951 two hundred stores now lined a thoroughfare that had none in 1939 (page 263).

Though most new suburban developments were overwhelmingly white and substantially residential, they were far from uniform. This 1951 aerial view shows the building of Fairless Hills—designed to house four thousand families of workers at the new Fairless Works of United States Steel—along U.S. Route 1 in lower Bucks County. The first of the prefabricated two- and three-bedroom ranchers went on sale in October 1952 for $10,000 and up, with as little as $411 down. Sited on 60- by 100-foot lots, the houses were loaded with new conveniences from all-electric kitchens to carports and built-in television antennas. Large picture windows were a special feature in Academy Gardens, a five-hundred-unit development just inside the Philadelphia line in Torresdale. In the 1950 view at right, above, a mother keeps a watchful eye on a child playing on the still-raw landscape of the new development. The picture window, a newly planted tree, and children at play within easy view of adults became symbols of the new suburban lifestyle. The 1962 view at right, of Springfield Township just across the Montgomery County line from Northwest Philadelphia, presents yet another kind of suburban scene. Developers here—building tract houses on old farms and estates—created an almost uniformly residential community. Like Academy Gardens and Fairless Hills, this was a refuge from work and a place to enjoy the new consumer society.

The suburbs offered many attractions: larger houses, open spaces, a refuge from work, and racial and class homogeneity. Their reputations as good places to bring up children were especially important, inextricably linking the postwar baby boom and the suburban expansion. The 1952 scene at the left of St. Dorothy's parish school in Drexel Hill was a common consequence. Opened only two years earlier as part of the expansion of Catholic education in eastern Delaware County, St. Dorothy's had already outgrown its eight schoolrooms and had moved some classes into the auditorium. New schools dotted the suburban landscape by the end of the decade. Below, students train in 1959 on the expansive athletic field shared by Springfield (Montgomery County) High School and Enfield Junior High School at Route 309 and Paper Mill Road. The building is typical of the low-lying, modern suburban school on a landscaped campus that was so attractive to parents and students when compared to the cramped school buildings of older city neighborhoods.

Levittown symbolized the new suburbs of the 1950s. After its first successful experimental development on Long Island, the Levitt Company began, in fall 1951, to build a more comprehensively planned community in lower Bucks County, only two miles from the Fairless steel complex. Mass-production techniques shown above rationalized construction into a 26-step process, allowing Levitt's workers to build a house every 16 minutes. The aerial view here, from Route 13 at the bottom of the picture, reveals the massive scale of the undertaking. When finished in 1958, the development encompassed 17,311 houses in 40 neighborhoods on 5,500 acres. All the houses were built as variations of a basic one-story ranch on a 75- by 100-foot lot. On page 270, we see a model living room in the Country Clubber, the most expensive house, which sold for $15,500 in 1954. A picture window—facing the backyard—stretched across the living and dining areas; Danish modern furniture (with one "colonial" chair) is arranged around the new television set. Levittown was an instant commercial triumph. Some of the thousands who jammed the site when the first houses went on view in December 1951 are shown on page 271. On that first weekend more than two hundred people put $100-deposits on ranch-style houses selling for as little as $9,990. Only six months later, and less than a year after the start of construction, the first families moved into Levittown.

Levittown developed into a prosperous community of blue-collar and white-collar workers and their families, with churches and synagogues, swimming pools, and a big shopping center. But there were growing pains. Above, the nearby Tullytown firehouse hosted classes in April 1953, when Levittown had thirty-seven hundred families, one supermarket, one drugstore, one restaurant, and no schools. As the newspaper caption pointed out, a curtain usually separated the children from the fire engines.

By the late 1950s, when many of the most pressing problems had been solved, each of the town's forty sections had its three to six hundred houses stretching along winding streets, with each street in a neighborhood starting with the same letter, so that people would not get lost among identical houses. With more than fifty thousand residents, the unincorporated development was divided among three townships. The community seemed to epitomize American success so well that there was talk of bringing Soviet Premier Nikita Khrushchev there on his American visit in the fall of 1959. On the facing page, the photographs of

the Vermillion Hills section, taken in anticipation of that event, are complete with such stereotypical images of contemporary suburban life as a man trimming his lawn with a power mower, a new Ford Fairlane (probably two-toned in a pastel color), and immature plants and shrubs. The photographs also convey some of the homogeneity of Levittown, which excluded the poor and blacks, the latter through official policy until 1959. In this, as in the more optimistic prohibition of fences between houses, Levittown embodied the America of the 1950s.

Though the metropolitan community of the 1950s remained concentrated around the city and the traditional industrial corridors, harbingers of a more dispersed Philadelphia were already present. Large shopping centers—dominated by immense parking lots—drew business from downtown and regional centers like Germantown Avenue. One of the more luxurious new centers was on the Bala Cynwyd side of City Line Avenue, between Belmont Avenue and Conshohocken State Road. Part of the fashion show marking the opening of the stores in September 1956 is shown here. (Note the skirt lengths.) The center had a department store—Lord & Taylor—aimed at the area's affluent residents, a supermarket, and about twenty-five other stores, ranging from Horn & Hardhart to Peck & Peck. A larger center opened in 1960 on the north side of Cheltenham Avenue—again just outside city limits—between Washington Lane and Ogontz Avenue. The Cheltenham Shopping Center (in the aerial view to the right) had been planned since 1953; the adjacent Gimbels (left center), then the largest in the Delaware Valley, had opened in 1955. The 62-acre tract, with parking for 4,500 cars, was strategically located at the end of the Fort Washington Expressway. The developers' claim that the center would draw people from a 20-mile radius emphasized the truly metropolitan sweep of such new shopping centers.

276

The area's new highways—though not so extensive or coordinated as those built in and around other large cities in the 1950s—laid the basis for the transformation of the metropolitan area in the following decades. The Schuylkill Expressway, under construction for the entire decade, was finally completed from the Walt Whitman Bridge to the Pennsylvania Turnpike in November 1959; as the 1960 scene opposite suggests, it was overcrowded and obsolete from its opening. A driver was lucky to average 20 miles per hour from the suburbs to center city in rush periods. Highways would have a more profound effect on the suburbs than on the city center. At King of Prussia, about 20 miles northwest of Center City, another powerful symbol of 1950s America had appeared on the ground in the shape of a cloverleaf where the Expressway met Route 202. First invented in the 1930s, the cloverleaf startled Americans who found it difficult to believe that you had to "turn right to go left." By the 1950s, however, the cloverleaf was no longer unusual, but the normal way to exit to the suburbs. When the view above was taken in 1954, King of Prussia was still in the countryside, but the future was equally obvious. Shopping and business centers had been planned, a motel built, and several housing developments were underway. Most local residents then worked in Philadelphia or in the industrial towns along the Schuylkill River. But by the end of the 1950s, a 700-acre King of Prussia industrial park boasted SKF, General Electric, Burroughs, and Sharp and Dohme plants. The automobile age was transforming King of Prussia into Philadelphia's rival for the commercial crown of the Delaware Valley.

The Spirit
of the
1950s

Set between the crises of Depression and war on one side and the turmoil of the 1960s on the other, the decade of the 1950s seems in retrospect a time of affluence, consensus, and complacency. The nation's emergence from World War II in a position of unquestioned global dominance and moral authority ushered in a golden age of sorts. More Americans than ever before shared in the national prosperity, and it was with an obvious relish that they turned to enjoying the fruits of their labor. In Philadelphia, as elsewhere, it was an age of television, suburbia, and babies; of rock and roll, bobbysocks, and cars with tailfins; of butterfly chairs, pole lamps, and outdoor barbecues. There were, to be sure, some lingering doubts, some hesitant voices in the national chorus of complacency. The A-Bomb and Sputnik were troubling facts of life; some Americans feared the Communist menace while others recoiled from McCarthyism and witch hunts. The decade also witnessed growing concerns about racial segregation, juvenile delinquency, and the corporate organization man.

A broadly based prosperity created an increasingly uniform national culture in the 1950s, making the experiences of many local residents much like those of their fellow Americans. Growing wealth led many white Philadelphians to the modern consumer paradise of area suburbs that, superficially at least, resembled their counterparts elsewhere. The decade's affluence touched others without disturbing older communities and traditions. For many who stayed in the city, better times could mean a washing machine or a vacuum cleaner delivered to one of the small rowhouses that continued to make Philadelphia different from other cities.

A consumer spending boom begun at war's end fueled the decade's prosperity. Americans scrambled to buy the appliances and automobiles that had been beyond the reach of most during the Depression and altogether unavailable during the war. By 1950, refrigerators were nearly universal in the city's working-class communities, and the ice-box was a memory even for most of Philadelphia's poor. Automatic washing machines, vacuum cleaners, frozen dinners, and Tupperware revolutionized housework in families with moderate means, but they may not have reduced the time women spent cooking and cleaning.

Not everyone benefited equally from the affluence of the 1950s. Blue-collar workers could expect steady work and wages at historically high levels, but with an average wage of $90 per week in 1960, Philadelphia factory workers could not purchase the full middle-class lifestyle. Average family income in the area rose over the course of the decade from $5,000 to about $7,000 per year,

The magic box, February 1950

but suburbanites made significantly more than city residents and whites much more than blacks. Most white families in such older neighborhoods as Kensington and South Philadelphia did not meet the $5,800 income level that the government calculated a family of four needed for a modestly comfortable lifestyle at the end of the decade. Of the city's two million inhabitants in 1960, about three hundred and fifty thousand fell below the poverty line and an equal number fell below the standard of modest comfort. And yet a clear majority of Philadelphians shared in the prosperity of the decade.

The automobile symbolized the abundance of the age. The number of cars registered in the city doubled to one-half million between 1945 and 1960. The rate of increase was even greater in the suburbs, where thousands of families found that they could not work, shop, or occupy their leisure time without a car or even two. Automobile ownership meant more venturesome vacations to distant places for some; cars returned to city and suburban streets sporting trophies in the form of decals from places like the Grand Canyon, Mammoth Cave, and Niagara Falls. For many working-class Philadelphians, the prosperity of the decade meant packing the kids into the car for a week- or even two-week-long vacation each year in the Poconos or at the Jersey shore. Attendance at Woodside, Willow Grove, and Riverside amusement parks declined as Philadelphians wandered more broadly afield in search of recreation; the trolleys and ferries connecting those sites to the city—like the parks themselves—soon became memories of innocent, bygone Sundays.

As cars became more necessary, they also became more ornate. Throughout the Delaware Valley, evenings and weekends were lavished on tending these elaborately grilled, pastel-shaded symbols of the new prosperity, a Chevrolet Impala, Mercury Montclair, or a Cadillac Eldorado. Yet Philadelphia did not become as dependent on cars as many newer metropolitan areas. Public transportation remained important—even the suburbs continued to depend on the Reading and Pennsylvania commuter rail lines—and the area developed only the most primitive highway system.

Equally symbolic of the decade's prosperity and its culture was television. Long a center of electronics research and manufacturing, Philadelphia was one of the first cities to participate fully in the communications revolution. The city's first stations—WPTZ, Channel 3; WFIL, Channel 6; and WCAU, Channel 10—began broadcasting shortly after the end of the war. Both major political parties selected Philadelphia for their national conventions in 1948, in part because its coaxial cable links to New York and Washington permitted millions of viewers in fourteen cities to see the nominating conventions on television. The new medium entered the city's homes with remarkable speed; one-third of Philadelphia households had television sets by 1950. The census that year revealed highest ownership rates not in the wealthiest parts of the city but in the semisuburban Northeast. Within another year, a majority of metropolitan Philadelphia households had the "magic box" and television was nearly universal by the end of the decade. Locally produced programs dominated 1950s airtime. "The Horn & Hardart Children's Hour" and "Chief Halftown" entertained youthful viewers; daytime fare included "The Girl Next Door" and "Pots, Pans, and Personalities"; while "Movie Quick Quiz" and "Mystery Star Quiz" were notable representatives of their genre. Ernie Kovacs displayed his manic comic brilliance in several short-running local programs. Movie attendance dropped dramatically from postwar highs, though the motion picture industry fought back with such innovations as Cinemascope and 3-D to retain its audiences. Radio had to adjust to a new and limited role as life in many homes came to center around a device few had heard of five years earlier.

Widespread automobile ownership and television programming ultimately transformed American life dramatically, but in the postwar period both served to reaffirm basic American values. The same was the case with the baby boom that began in 1946 and continued through the 1950s. By 1950, there were almost two hundred thousand children—or more than 10 percent of the population —five years old and under in Philadelphia. In the even more child-centered suburbs by 1960 over one-third of the residents were eighteen and under. The baby boom reverberated endlessly throughout the 1950s, stimulating demand for everything from baby food and living space to Sugar Pops and Davy Crockett caps. New elementary and high schools by the score appeared across the region; the city's tight-fisted Board of Education even consented to build new high schools in the growing Northeast—Lincoln in 1950 and Northeast in 1958.

The age group making the most special mark on the 1950s was teenagers. They staked their claim primarily through their music, an adaptation of black popular music that offended and disturbed many white adults even as it exhilarated their teenaged offspring. Philadelphia had long been a center for both white and black popular music. Despite blue laws that restricted Sunday drinking to private clubs until 1960, nightclubs like the Latin Casino and jazz bars like Billy Kretchemer's and the Blue Note attracted talented musicians to the area throughout the 1950s. Home to such early rock and roll pioneers as Lee Andrews and the Hearts, and Bill Haley and the Comets, the Philadelphia area provided appreciative and enthusiastic young fans. The cheaply produced 45 rpm record, which first appeared in 1949 and soon became the standard for popular hits, stimulated the spread of rock and roll.

In Philadelphia, teenagers and television combined with popular music to produce "American Bandstand," the city's great contribution to the popular culture of the age. Bandstand started in 1952 as a local television version of the radio music shows; the program invited white teens in to dance at the WFIL studios in the old Arena at 46th and Market Streets in order to have something to screen while the music played. When the show switched from traditional pop music to the much less respectable rock and roll, it became a sensation. By 1957 Bandstand was being telecast nationally for ninety minutes each weekday afternoon. Millions rushed home from schools across the country to watch and emulate kids from Little Flower, West Philadelphia Catholic, and other local schools. To be a regular like Kenny, Arlene, Bob, or Justine was nearly the ultimate in teenaged aspiration.

Bandstand rock and roll was relatively tame. Teens needed passes to get on the show and some lied about their ages. Adult Philadelphia, however, rarely perceived Bandstand as threatening social peace and traditional morality. They reserved that kind of hostility for the uncompromising black rock that many white teens found attractive. Georgie Woods, whose Philadelphia career as a disc jockey began in 1953, drew large white audiences to black-oriented radio stations WHAT and WDAS. Woods also brought black rock to mixed crowds at center city's Mastbaum and West Philadelphia's Nixon theaters.

The publicity about juvenile delinquency and gangs also worried parents. The city imposed a late-night curfew in 1955, barring youths under seventeen from the streets. There were some nasty incidents—a young man making a bank deposit at Broad and Fairmount died in the crossfire between warring gangs in 1956—but the Moroccans, Seybert Streeters, Villagers, White Caps, and other teenaged gangs were usually less violent than they tried to appear. Throughout the city it was more common for residents to walk the streets in the evening without fearing for their personal safety than it would be in later decades. Crimes like homicide, robbery, larceny, and auto theft were actually less common in Philadelphia in 1960 than they had been at the end of the Korean War in 1953.

The anxieties that the massive numbers of baby-boom teenagers aroused in adult Philadelphians were nonetheless real. Seeking to gain control over their children and at the same time responding to the family-oriented and child-centered values of the period, adults expanded such supervised activities as Scouting, school sports, chaperoned hops, and other wholesome fun. Little Leagues became fixtures in the emerging suburban landscape; in the city, public-spirited citizens cooperated with the police in the Police Athletic League. Local station houses sponsored P.A.L. competitions in baseball, football, basketball, and boxing, enrolling such future stars as Sonny Liston, Joe Frazier, and Wilt Chamberlain as well as more ordinary athletes. In addition to the positive influences brought to bear on the youth generation, parents and schools had considerably greater powers of compulsion available to them in the 1950s than later generations of adults would have. Bible reading and dress codes were the rule of the day in Philadelphia schools. Only the most minimal legal rights limited adult authority over the behavior of young people.

Other fears were less amenable to control. By the beginning of the decade, with the nation at war in Korea, near-hysteria over the twin threats of nuclear war and Communism gripped the country. Many found reassurance in a renewed patriotism, of which the increased attention paid to historic shrines was one manifestation. Plans to set Independence Hall within a parklike mall—to exalt the old State House as a central shrine of America's republican faith—had their origins in World War II but were finally realized in the Cold War atmosphere of the 1950s.

But there was also a darker side to that patriotic fervor. McCarthyism and the myriad witch hunts for spies and subversives left bleak monuments in Philadelphia every bit as palpable as Independence National Historic Park. Political groups and unions purged members suspect because of left-wing sentiments. The toll in the local schools was particularly high. While no more than two dozen teachers and several university professors were fired for invoking constitutional rights in front of investigatory panels, freedom of speech itself was the primary victim. The red scare instilled fear, chilling political discussion and restricting artistic expression for the entire decade. It was against this background that Philadelphia's business and political elite made their plans to rebuild the city, plans that sometimes demolished entire neighborhoods without arousing significant protest from communities too frightened to defend their interests.

A growing fear of nuclear annihilation punctuated this enforced complacency. Air-raid drills, civil defense programs, and black-and-yellow fallout shelter signs reminded Philadelphians of the threat from Russian guided missiles. After Sputnik orbited in 1957, no one doubted that Philadelphia—with its shipyards, refineries, electronics industry, arsenal, and nearby military bases— was high on the list of Russian targets.

It was through the fears of the 1950s that Philadelphians entered the insecure modern world. In retrospect, however, it is noteworthy that many of the city's residents managed to cling to older ways of life and traditional values even through the dramatic transitions of the decade. The affluent society of suburban tract houses, two-car garages, and frozen dinners had spread unevenly across the Delaware Valley, touching down fairly lightly in the city's rowhouse neighborhoods and in the region's smaller industrial cities. Perhaps more than any other significant concentration of Americans in the period, Philadelphians continued to live in ethnically defined communities, where historic loyalties continued to hold many of the old communities together. Old habits died hard in neighborhoods where the communal experiences of stoop-sitting and street games competed successfully with the self-imposed isolation of evenings devoted to television viewing.

The automobile culture—with its shopping centers and drive-ins—inevitably had only a limited impact in crowded city streets. The city itself remained largely segregated, its racial tensions barely concealed and sometimes exploding in conflict as blacks moved into previously all-white communities or jobs. Philadelphia's black and white cultures were separate, brought together only sporadically by the spread of black music into white popular culture and the reverse spread of white television into the black community. Yet in the decade immediately before the racially troubled and violent 1960s, white working-class South Philadelphia had as much in common with black working-class West Philadelphia as it did with the new white middle-class suburbs. The white teenagers from rowhouse neighborhoods dancing to essentially black music for a national television audience on American Bandstand provide an appropriately complex symbol for 1950s Philadelphia.

The 1950s dream of a consumer paradise seemed to be coming true for many Philadelphians. Though carefully staged, these photographs convey the postwar prosperity enjoyed by many white middle-class families. Here, a photograph of a neighborhood barbecue in Germantown, taken to illustrate a 1950 story in *McCall's* magazine, represents the good life and the traditional values of home, family, and privacy.

The technological miracles, which unfolded throughout the decade, are illustrated on the next page in a 1954 view of the fully modernized kitchen belonging to Mrs. Gregory Gibson of Fairy Hill Road in Jenkintown. From the round fluorescent lights and the dishwasher to the refrigerator-freezer and the electric range, the room boasts of the wonders of the age.

The children of the 1950s were beneficiaries of the broadly shared belief that children deserved the best—from good public schools to endless consumer goods—that their parents could provide. The consumer society was perfectly suited to the desires and demands of children; their heroes and symbols came to dominate American culture. The new medium of television created Howdy Doody, who started his thirteen-year run in 1947. Above, he presides over a watermelon-eating contest held as part of the *Bulletin*'s sixth annual Fairmount Park Fourth of July celebration in 1950.

Staffed by a corps of talented and underpaid women who had followed a traditional path into teaching, the city's public schools generally gave students a solid if conservative education in the basics. On the following page (top), Emily Stopper teaches her first grade reading group at the Harrington School at 53rd and Baltimore in 1955. Despite the benefits of such attention, children were always happy to welcome the summer vacation. (Below) the last day of school has come at the McCall School, at 7th and Delancey, in June 1953. As the photograph makes clear, the school —in a long time immigrant and black neighborhood—was integrated, as it always had been. The picture at Harrington presaged a different story. Though the city's public schools were one-third black by 1955, the class was all white. Within ten years, the student body at Harrington would be virtually all black.

The fear of communism and the threat of nuclear war darkened the postwar years. The *Bulletin* ran the photograph at the right on December 8, 1950, under the headline "School Children Drill for Possible A-Bomb Attack." These children at the Morrison School at 3rd and Duncannon were told that they would be protected from a nuclear bomb by remaining inside the building and covering their heads. "Duck and cover" scenes were reenacted across the nation in the early 1950s; they remain an indelible symbol of the period. The evacuation of center city on the morning of November 23, 1954, shown below, was a similarly odd exercise. Code-named "Operation Scram," the prearranged drill began when civil defense sirens called more than twenty-five thousand office and municipal workers in the area between Broad and 17th and Race and Market Streets away from work. Led by Mayor Joseph Clark, thousands marched up the Parkway to the designated assembly area at 21st Street, where, in a real emergency, they would board transport out of the city. Everyone agreed that the mass evacuation—the first in any large American city—had been a great success. But as the decade proceeded, the futility of such exercises gradually became apparent.

The expansion of television transformed daily life more rapidly and more completely than movies or radio had; by about 1950, newspapers were covering the social change as an ongoing story. The rush to join the revolution had become a stampede by the time of the February 1950 television sale at Wanamaker's documented here at the top left. Factories worked overtime to turn out sets like the 16-inch model displayed. Though the $190 price represented about half a month's income for the average family, there were half a million sets in the Philadelphia metropolitan area by the end of 1950. Broadcasters rushed to fill the airwaves.

At the left, the 16th and Chestnut Street studio of WCAU-TV, the *Bulletin*-owned CBS affiliate, telecasts a home economics show in October 1950. Such unadorned local programming sufficed for daytime television in the early years, when simply watching the screen was a special event. In May 1949, the *Bulletin* had already reported how television was changing family life in Philadelphia. Watch-

ing television here is the DiPalma family of Overbrook. Future movie director Brian DiPalma is the child at the far right engrossed in the "Bar 10 Ranch." There was widespread agreement that television was becoming the center of daily life for many, that families were rearranging their homes and schedules to accommodate it, and that the medium brought the world into the home. One fan told the *Bulletin* in 1949 that television was "insurance against ever being alone."

Television and youth culture came together in the Bandstand program. The original master of ceremonies, radio disc jockey Bob Horn, had livened up the video version of his show by asking conventionally groomed teenagers to come in and dance a mild "jitterbug" to respectable popular music for the cameras. The song titles in July 1955 shown in the photograph above indicate that Bandstand pointedly ignored the growing popularity of rock and roll. With the community in an uproar over juvenile delinquency and "Negro" rock and roll, Horn kept his show a model of respectability. When Horn left the show in 1956, WPVI-TV brought in twenty-seven-year old Dick Clark, shown on the opposite page, who opened the show to the new rock and roll; in July 1957, Bandstand went to national distribution and became American Bandstand. The show reflected American society. Though it came from a city one-quarter black, was located in a primarily black neighborhood, played music that was generally black in derivation, and even broke new ground in commonly featuring black performers, all of the dancers shown here are white, and the Bandstand club was virtually all white. This did not pass unnoticed; there was a small disturbance in October 1957 when black teenagers were kept out of a performance by black entertainer Bobby Brooks. A gradual and grudging integration followed. Through it all, the show remained immensely popular with teenagers and their younger siblings from across the social and ethnic spectrum.

The city's street games and street life represented continuity more than innovation. To the left, the 800 block of North Lawrence Street, near 4th and Poplar, is shown in March 1953. Many Eastern European Jewish immigrants and their descendants lived in this white, working-class neighborhood. Teenaged cardplayers below, left, mugged cooperatively for the Housing Association photographer at the corner of Hope and Turner Streets, near Front and Oxford, in 1957. Both photographs document the survival of familiar street life in the television age. The newer youth culture is evident here in the strictly supervised Teen Canteen at suburban Elkins Park Junior High School in October 1955. Though such events were well known for girls dancing with one another while boys looked on awkwardly, this scene reveals a number of couples trying out steps possibly learned from a television program like Bandstand.

In the tightly knit rowhouse communities of the older city, Philadelphia's traditional ways of life remained vibrant. Adults and children alike followed familiar routines and enjoyed familiar pleasures. People met friends and neighbors, gossiped, played, and did their chores on familiar streets. With air-conditioning virtually unknown in working-class houses, warm weather saw the streets fill with neighborhood social life, some of the flavor of which these photographs convey. Below, a bocce score is calculated in South Philadelphia in 1951; the distance between the large balls—the boules—and the small round jack is measured with a metal rod or baguette. With its small court and non-grass playing surface, bocce was a perfect urban game. At right, the interior of Pflaumer's Ice Cream parlor in Strawberry Mansion is shown in 1951. For decades, Pflaumer's had been at 33rd and Ridge across from Fairmount Park, in a predominantly Jewish community. On page 298, John Mosley, a black commercial photographer, depicts residents talking to a workman in one of the more prosperous sections of North Philadelphia in the late 1950s. In the last photograph, Mrs. Helen Parise spends Labor Day 1959 mending baby clothes while her son cools off on the 2900 block of North Bonsall Street, near 23rd and Indiana, in what was then a predominantly Italian community. Clearly, much of the texture and variety of city life had survived the changes of the 1950s.

Formal organizations and gatherings also carried on the traditional popular culture of the city. Mummers' parades, as the January 2, 1950 revelry (above) on Second Street revealed, changed little. Though blackface was offensive to blacks, it did not become an open issue until the 1960s. On the next page, members of the Loyal Orange Institute celebrate the Orange victory over Ireland's Catholics in the 1690 Battle of the Boyne. Five hundred marchers from twenty-three lodges and twelve women's auxiliaries participated in this 1947 parade. Unlike the St. Patrick's Day parade of the city's much larger Irish Catholic community, this procession passed through Fairmount Park rather than through residential areas where trouble might break out. On page 301, top, a large crowd attends the fifteenth annual Easter Sunrise Service at Broad and Roosevelt in April 1950. Below, the children of St. Adalbert's parish march along Chestnut Street in the annual Polish parade in 1948. Many of the city's eastern European Catholics, like many of its eastern European Jews, were only a generation or two removed from immigration in the 1950s. With the added trauma of the wartime and postwar experiences of their homelands, ethnic consciousness remained high.

Prosperity and growing leisure time expanded the position of sports in American popular culture. Professional sports further benefited from the rise of television; by the end of the decade, television exposure had promoted professional football into a national pastime almost the equal of baseball. Despite the loss of the Athletics team to Kansas City in 1955, Philadelphia remained very much a baseball town throughout the decade. There was nearly universal excitement in 1950 when the Phillies unexpectedly won the National League pennant for the first time since 1915. Here, fans line up at Shibe Park to buy tickets for the World Series opener, which the Phillies unhappily lost 1 to 0 on the way to a four-game sweep by the Yankees. The importance of sports in the 1950s was even more obvious at the high school level. Schools encouraged student sports as a healthy alternative to other adolescent amusements; school sports also gave teenagers a collective identity that was supposed to reduce class, race, and ethnic divisions. In newer suburbs, where few other traditions existed, high school sports often served as a community's strongest common bond. School sports everywhere were designed to reinforce commonly accepted gender roles: boys played, girls cheered. To the right, above, Overbrook High School cheerleaders agonize over their team's loss in the March

1950 city basketball championship game against unbeaten LaSalle, led by Tom Gola. The city series had begun in 1939; sixty-five hundred fans witnessed the 1950 game at the Palestra. Football—the other major high school sport—also had a following in the thousands in many communities. Below, Radnor beats Lower Merion, 47 to 14, at Villanova Stadium on Thanksgiving weekend, 1958. The crowd of ten thousand emphasized the continuing vitality of school sports in the 1950s, at a time when the professional Eagles and Warriors languished in relative obscurity.

Even as the suburban ideal of privacy took hold, and home television viewing replaced more communal pastimes, downtown Philadelphia remained the site of some important public entertainments. Above, excited crowds wait outside the Earle Theater at 11th and Market in March 1953 to purchase tickets for a performance by Johnnie Ray, an enormously popular crooner in the years just before rock and roll. As with some later rock and roll idols, the emotional singing and accompanying stage gyrations of the "Prince of Wails" sent many female "bobby-soxers" into ecstasy, and elicited disapproving comments from some adults. To the right above, is the "Little Engine That Could" chugging down Broad Street trailing cars full of chocolate, lollipops, and soda in the 1954 Gimbel's Thanksgiving Day parade, a more traditional spectacle celebrating the consumer society. In contrast to later parades, the forty floats and five thousand marchers started at Broad and Montgomery in the heart of residential North Philadelphia. Half a million people—one of the largest crowds in the thirty-four-year history of the event—witnessed the 1954 parade. Motorcades featuring visiting officials were also regular downtown rituals; politicians and other notables traveled in open cars with little apparent concern for security. In the last picture, Vice-President Richard Nixon—a powerful symbol of 1950s America—travels from Reyburn Plaza to Independence Hall on July 4, 1953, to give a speech attacking the Soviet Union. It is unclear whether the photographer intentionally juxtaposed the Vice-President and the movie marquee behind him. The film about the dark side of science, like the Vice-President's speech, is a reminder of some of the strains in the smiling face of the 1950s.

Sources

Abbreviations

Bul   *Evening Bulletin* photograph collections, Urban Archives Center, Temple University

HADV   Housing Association of Delaware Valley collection, Urban Archives Center, Temple University

HSP   Historical Society of Pennsylvania

Inq   *Philadelphia Inquirer* photograph collections, Urban Archives Center, Temple University

LC   Library of Congress

NA   National Archives (RG indicates Record Group)

PHMC   Pennsylvania Historical and Museum Commission

Rec   *Philadelphia Record* collection, Historical Society of Pennsylvania

UA   Urban Archives Center, Temple University Libraries

WPA   WPA Pennsylvania Guide project photographs, RG13, Pennsylvania Historical and Museum Commission

Note: If there are two or more photographs on a page, the references below begin with either the top or the leftmost photograph on the page, and are separated by a comma. If a range of pages is indicated, then all the photographs within that range came from one source.

Introduction: A City in Transition

2 Atwater Kent Museum; 7 Bul; 8 Rec; 9 NA–RG306; 10 Bul, WPA; 11 Rec; 12 Bul; 13 Rec; 14 HSP–Penrose collection; 15 HADV; 16 Meyer Sherow; 17 David Cherry; 18 Free Library of Philadelphia; 19 Rec, Meyer Sherow; 21 PHMC—Highway Department; 22 HSP—Wallace collection; 23 UA—Regional Planning Federation collection, Rec; 24 UA–City Parks Association collection; 25 NA–RG30; 26 Rec; 27 WPA; 28 LC; 29 Bul; 30 Rec; 31 Inq; 32–33 WPA; 34 Rec; 35 WPA (both); 36–39 Bul; 40 WPA; 41 Bul, Rec

The Knife of the Depression

42 Rec; 48–50 Bul; 51 Rec; 52 Bul; 53 Inq; 54 Rec; 55 Rec, Inq; 56 WPA; 57 Rec; 58 Bul (both); 59 LC; 60 WPA (both); 61 NA–RG69, Inq; 62 WPA; 63 WPA, NA–RG69; 64 Rec; 65 Bul; 66 Rec; 67 Meyer Sherow, Inq; 68 Rec; 69 Bul; 70 Bul (both); 71–73 Rec

Family Album, 1920s and 1930s

74 David and Elsie Kendis, Mr. and Mrs. George Moore, Jr.; 75 David and Elsie Kendis, Kerry Krieger; 76 Michael Dever, Marjorie Poole; 77 Bowser collection–Balch Institute for Ethnic Studies, Mrs. Garrett Magens; 78 Ruth Vodges, Lila Luber, Marguerite DePaul; 79 Shirley Adler; 80 Meyer Sherow (both); 81 Pat Stopper, Samuel Salzman, John Clifton

The New Deal City

82 Bul; 88 Rec; 89 NA–RG306, Bul; 90–91 Bul; 92 Bul, NA–RG195; 93 WPA (both); 94–95 NA–RG196; 96 NA–RG119 (both); 97 Bul, Inq; 98 Rec, WPA; 99 NA–RG69 (both); 100 NA–RG306; 101 Inq (both); 102–104 Rec; 105 Inq (both); 106 Rec, Bul; 107 Rec; 109 NA–RG306; 110 Rec; 111 Bul

Homefront

112 Rec; 118–119 Bul; 120 Inq; 121 Inq, Bul; 122 LC (both); 123 Inq; 124–126 LC; 127 Bul; 128 Rec; 130 UA–NAACP collection; 131 Rec (both); 132–133 Inq; 134–135 Bul; 136 Rec, Inq; 137 Bul; 138–141 Inq; 142 Rec, Inq; 143 Bul (both); 144 Inq, HADV; 145 HADV (both); 146 Inq; 147 Rec; 148 Inq; 149 Bul, Inq; 150 Rec (both); 151 Inq

Family Album, World War II

152 Charles Tompkins, Betty Jenkins; 153 David and Elsie Kendis, Evelyn Robinson, David and Elsie Kendis; 154 Ruth Kramer, Wilma Pitkapaasi; 155 Mary Grace and Ted Gilmore, Mrs. Thomas Bentz; 156 Betty Jenkins, Marjorie Poole; 157 F. J. McWilliams, Sophie Brooks, Kerry Krieger

A Last Hurrah

158 Bul; 164–165 Inq; 166 Bul; 167–187 Inq; 188 NA–RG306, Inq; 189 Inq

The Enduring Rowhouse City

190 Rec; 195 Rec, Bul; 196 Bul; 197–198 NA–RG306; 199 Inq; 200 Bul; 201 UA–Germantown Community Council collection; 202 Inq; 203 Bul; 204–205 Bul; 206 Robert Weidenbaker, Rec; 207 Philadelphia City

Archives; 208–209 Bul; 210–215 HADV; 216 HADV, Bul; 217 Bul; 218 Inq; 219–221 Bul; 222 Diane McGonigle; 223–224 Bul; 226 NA Philadelphia Branch–RG181; 227 Bul

Family Album, 1945–1960

228 Mosley collection–Charles L. Blockson Afro-American Collection at Temple University, Wilma Pitkapaasi; 229 Michael Dever; 230 Mr. and Mrs. Gilbert Shipman, Sherry Nelson; 231 Mosley collection–Blockson Collection, Sophie Brooks; 232 Mosley collection–Blockson Collection; 233 Adam and Joanne Gargani, Mary Grace and Ted Gilmore; 234 Michael Dever, Diane McGonigle; 235 Marjorie Poole, Mrs. Thomas Bentz; 236 Barbara Klaczynska, Mary Branigan; 237 Mary Grace and Ted Gilmore; 238 Aram Aghazarian; 239 Wilma Pitkapaasi, Dellie Rosen

Metropolis Reshaped

240 NA–RG306; 247 Bul; 248 NA–RG306; 249 Philadelphia City Archives; 250 HADV, Bul; 251 HADV; 252–253 Bul; 254–255 HADV; 256 Bul; 257 Inq; 258 Bul; 259–260 Inq; 261 Philadelphia City Archives; 262–263 Bul; 264 Inq; 265–268 Bul; 269 NA–RG306; 270 HADV; 271–276 Bul; 277 Inq

The Spirit of the 1950s

278 Bul; 285 NA–RG306; 286 Bul; 287 NA–RG306; 288–293 Bul; 294 HADV (both); 295–297 Bul; 298 Mosley collection–Blockson Collection, Inq; 299 Inq; 300 Inq; 301 Bul, Inq; 302–304 Inq; 305 Bul, UA–Phillips collection

Index